Of Sun and Sand

Edited by: A.J. Huffman
and April Salzano

Cover Art by A.J. Huffman

Copyright © 2013 A.J. Huffman

All rights reserved. Except for brief quotations in critical articles or reviews, no part of this book may be reproduced in any manner without prior written permission from the publisher:

Kind of a Hurricane Press
www.kindofahurricanepress.com
kindofahurricanepress@gmail.com

CONTENTS

April Salzano	*Sifting through the Sand*	11
	From The Poets	
Pamela Ahlen	*Seascape*	15
Barbara Bald	*Musings at Fort McClary*	17
	The Jailor	18
Linda Bearss	*Adirondacks on the Sand*	19
James Bell	*Bracklesham Sands*	20
Byron Beynon	*Surfers*	21
	Seaweed	22
	Cefn Sidan	23
Doug Bolling	*Wanting it All*	24
	Going to China	25
Nancy Brashear	*I Want Him Not*	28
Bob Brill	*What the Sea Gives Back*	30
	Beach Sonata	31
Michael H. Brownstein	*The Season of Tropical Irregularities*	33
Lesley Burt	*At Cavelossim*	34
	Do Not Drown	35
Fern G.Z. Carr	*Resenting Dead Fish*	36

Beth Copeland	*Afterlife*	37
Linda M. Crate	*I Need Your Beach*	38
Chris Crittenden	*Bricks on the Beach*	39
Betsey Cullen	*Sun Beach, Vieques*	40
Oliver Cutshaw	*Santa Monica Pier*	41
Susan Dale	*July, 07*	43
	Comes Time	44
Jessica de Koninck	*Solstice*	46
	This Boardwalk Life	47
Hannah Dellabella	*Peaking*	48
	Nature in a Crowded State	49
Darren C. Demaree	*Without Thread, Here, We are Connected to Everything*	50
Laura Dennis	*September*	51
Andrea Janelle Dickens	*After Crabbing*	52
	Hatteras Evacuation	53
	Sargasso	56
Richard Dyer	*Sand, My Old Friend*	57
Jim Eigo	*Sheer as the Water Itself*	59
Will Falk	*A Natural Event*	61
Kate Falvey	*Divertimento for Sea and Sunscreen*	62

Alexis Rhone Fancher	*Sibling Rivalry*	63
Elysabeth Fasland	*Sun and Sand . . . 'Flip Side'*	65
Richard Fein	*Mining for China*	66
Joan Fishbein	*Before*	67
Neil Flatman	*15 Years Later in Morrow Bay*	69
Trina Gaynon	*Sand Surfing*	70
Katie Hopkins Gebler	*Pages of Instruction Go Unread*	72
Sue Mayfield Geiger	*Fire Bird*	73
Patricia L. Goodman	*Fragments*	75
Zélie Guérin	*Where Gods Encircle and Sins Recite*	76
Deborah Guzzi	*The Sandy Shoal*	78
	Sea Food	79
Judy Hall	*Back the Way I Came*	80
	The Intertidal Zone	81
Dave Hardin	*Stars from North Manitou*	83
William Ogden Haynes	*A Bit of Summer in Winter*	84
Damien Healy	*Ocean Day*	86
William D. Hicks	*My World*	87
Christopher Hivner	*Holy Ocean Sonata*	88
	Shifting	90

	I Am a Bronze God	91
Liz Hufford	One More Summer at the Shore	92
S.E. Ingraham	A Beach Stained Indigo	94
M.J. Iuppa	Genesis	95
Miguel Jacq	Sirens	96
	Sydney	97
Michael Lee Johnson	While the Seashells Listen, I Love You	98
	In December	99
	Lost in a Distant Harbor	100
Caroline Jones	Beach Scene	101
Judith J. Katz	Summer in the City	102
	Who Has Such Phenomena in His World	103
	Green Sky at Night	104
Claire Keyes	Einstein at the Beach	106
	Kayaking the Sakonnet	107
	After the Hurricane	109
Steve Klepetar	A Sail	110
Craig Kyzar	Adrift	111
Kate LaDew	Those Mornings on the Beach	113
Duane Locke	Terrestrial Illuminations No. 545	114

Michael Magee	*Volare 1955*	115
	Solzhenitsyn at the Beach	117
Jacqueline Markowski	*On the Coast*	118
	Places to Go and Places Not to Go	120
Carolyn Martin	*Three's*	121
Austin McCarron	*Across Graves of Sand*	122
Joan McNerney	*Neptune's Coquette*	123
Karla Linn Merrifield	*Beach Tao*	124
	The Truth of Florida's Living Beaches	125
	Seeking Heaven: Why I Collect Seashells	127
Claudia Messelodi	*At the Seaside*	129
Les Merton	*Mahdia Beach*	130
John Miatech	*Inverness*	131
	How Things End	132
	Place of Great Water	133
George Moore	*The Boats*	134
Joseph Murphy	*Along the Beach*	135
James B. Nicola	*(untitled)*	136
Christine Nichols	*Siren's Call*	137
George H. Northrup	*Beach Religion*	139

	Ram's Head Island: New Ears for New Music	140
Bret Norwood	Black Sand Beach	141
Jennifer Ostromecki	Buried Treasure	142
Carl Palmer	Mirage	144
Stephen V. Ramey	Fishing	145
kerry rawlinson	Ocean	146
Nina Romano	Beach Tide Pool	148
	Swimming	149
Eva Schlesinger	Beach Therapy	151
J.lynn Sheridan	Beaches	152
	Reading into Summer	153
Tamara Simpson	The Bar	155
Tom Sterner	Questioning Horsery	157
Chris Stiebens	Suddenly Sunday	159
Emily Strauss	Inner Landscapes	160
	Crush of Waves	161
Bonnie Quan Symons	Tropical Tempest	162
Marianne Szlyk	Seaweed on the Beach	163
	Find Your Beach Where It Is	164
Terence Thomas	Sand Man	166

Tim Tobin	A Waltz on the Beach	169
Christine Tsen	Yankee Iron – ee cummings	172
	Jawing	173
Mercedes Webb-Pullman	Kovalenko's Zen	175
	Self-Serve	177
Anne Whitehouse	Scenes from California	178
	A Girl Who Fell in Love with an Island	180
	Songs for the End of August	181
John Sibley Williams	Nostalgia	183
	Holiday	184
Martin Willitts, Jr.	Tarot: Moon with Water and Crab	185
Matthew Wylie	On Entering	186
	A Few Words Near the Boardwalk and a Star	188
	A Few Questions for the Ocean	190
Robert Wynne	Reflection: After the Great Wave	191
	Bolsa Chica State Beach	192
	One Red Umbrella	193
Ron Yanzinski	Amelia Island	194
	Off Key West, Hemmingway Sails with Homer	195

Mantz Yorke	*Freshfield Beach*	196
	From The Editors	
A.J. Huffman	*Heliophile*	199
	Red Tide	200
	The Fishermen	201
	There is Something Wrong	202
	Squirrels on the Beach	203
April Salzano	*A Woman on the Beach that is Now a Stranger*	204
	Dragging the Ocean	205
	Bathtub Conclusions	206
	My Kids Think Lake Erie is the Ocean	207
	Remains	208
	Author Bios	211
	About the Editors	233

Sifting through the Sand

I confess that I was intimidated, on several levels, when Amy proposed this particular theme. Maybe skeptical is a better word. A true northerner, I have visited a handful of beaches, but never felt particularly attached to the ocean the way other writers have described, the way Amy undoubtedly is in Florida with the beach as her back yard. I did not think I would be able to come up with poetry about the beach that would say anything particularly original.

My other thought was that we would be inundated with redundancy. I feared everyone would write about the pull of the water, the humbling effect of the ocean, sand between toes, and maybe a few vacation poems. I would like to say I have never been so happy to be wrong. The work we received for this anthology certainly has a common thread, but the diversity was a pleasant surprise.

We received some of what we expected, however those particular poems were anything but cliché. In addition, we received interpretations of the theme that I never would have predicted: frozen beaches, oceans ripe with mythology and metaphor, sandcastles and fish, surfing with mermaids…many from northerners like myself, who seem to have a different take on water than the ocean-natives, whose pieces evoke a sense of familiarity and a kind of claim to the ocean uniquely belonging to those who play in the sand more frequently. The voices in this anthology are as distinct as seashells, and just as beautifully crafted. The writers addressed every imaginable aspect of this theme, and then dived in deeper to uncover even more buried treasures.

We hope our readers are as inspired and impressed by the work featured in this anthology as we are.

From The Poets

Seascape

At the edge of sea to shining
beneath the spacious sky,
the brotherhood of fishing poles and SCV's,
big beach covered in best buy,
sea filled with American Dreams.

*

Near the wrinkled rose
and the bench marked
Yet We But Borrow the Land
the artist paints pink stain sky,
a white daub of saltbox house,
smears of oil-slick tide.

*

Charlie builds castles on sand,
develops the shore
and offends the land,
his need to greed
persistent as the riptide sea.

*

She paddles past *Belinda's* bow,
the gull patrolling *Brenda's* stern,
paddles across the cove and skirts the stone bank –
paying homage to graying skiffs
clumped together like forgotten fishwives,
unnamed ladies bobbing mute, their secrets in repose.

*

We spend our lives
out of water,

fish treading
dryland shore.
Here at the sea
we've come home,
lungs to gills and arms to fins,
floating the sweet-salt sea
on pink rubber ducks,
green manatees.

-- Pamela Ahlen

Musings at Fort McClary

Clustered like chess pieces ready for the next game,
moored by multi-colored buoys that resemble
juju beads in a flat tub, masts jut upward from the harbor.

Sails wrapped mummy-like in blue canvas
rock contentedly in the wake of a more ambitious captain.
Their lines, paralleled and angled, form a mosaic of triangles,
half-moons and rectangles.

What stories hide in their hulls?
What honeymoon whispers? Retired dreams?

Vessels rest in the noonday sun, too hot to travel,
too hazy to sight a clear route, yet
like spaniels waiting for the word *ride*,
each craft stands ready for the next journey.

Do they anticipate future escapades
or envy canary-colored kayaks that sleek by?

Do ships keep tactile scrapbooks? Long for first captains?
Harbor secrets they wished they'd shared?
Perhaps age makes a difference –
young ones poised to spring into the next adventure,
older craft content to await the next sunset.

On shore, white-ash shade accentuates cool inlet breezes.
Staccato cries of gulls punctuate the drone of a weed-eater,
preening the park for new arrivals.

Dog-day afternoons absorb energy like a sponge,
put projects on hold, replace productivity
with deep breaths and even pulses.

-- Barbara Bald

The Jailor

The beach speaks in low tones, an off-season lull.
Spreading towel on sands waiting for summer's sun,
I position my chair facing the water's edge.
Towel neatly folded, sunscreen calling,
I place my book beside the mat.

Near me a chipmunk scoots through crevices
in granite walls that line the shore.
He darts in and out in playful fashion,
stuffed cheeks sizing up the scene.

Diapers and swimsuit left behind,
a baby girl toddles to the water's edge.
Wide eyes fixed on a black lab sharing her tub,
she plops bare-bottom on wet sand.

The spunky lab, tail, beating like a metronome,
leaps from spring waters; two sticks flying high
make his day.

I wish I could slide into holes full of mystery,
wish I could abandon suit and beach shoes,
not worry if sands are shifting, holes are dark or
that I might miss the stick.

I want to lift, ears flapping in total bliss, but
when risk is the enemy, prison bars erect themselves.
Over time, walls of a familiar house, a favorite shirt,
even mocha lattes, ordered again and again,
become self-appointed wardens.

The beach sign should read, *Habits that start as cobwebs can end up as cables.* Security can become the jailor who guards the keys.

-- Barbara Bald

Adirondacks on the Sand

Tall and broad, he deposits himself gingerly in the damp Adirondack,
determined not to disturb the silence that has wrapped her in faded
fleece and memories, a cotton candy sunrise. She loves the sunrise,
the whisper of the waves washing the night's harvest from the sand
 and rocks. She finds her words again.

He speaks quietly, "I knew I'd find you here."
She peeks up from under the hat's cotton brim,
drawing her lips into a delicate crescent.

"Maybe," he philosophizes, "this is one box you dive into.
Maybe, women have just a box or two
where they dive in and hide away, untangled."

The gulls notice the new comer and waddle across the sand,
side to side like children's weighted, plastic clowns that fall and rise,
fall and rise, painted smiles at constant garish attention. They watch
the man and woman, waiting for crumbs or stones.

The woman's wiring unkinks, loosens, and she sees
the thing clearly – a moment on a quiet stretch of sand,
a sunrise, a warm cup of coffee, and her notebook.
She senses the chilled, dewy beads on her cheeks,
the sand's grit on the arm of the chair beneath her finger tips.
Stretching, she unties the precious package, now for two.

"You're right," she meets his eyes and smiles softly.

Sunlight spreads over her jeans and ancient college sweatshirt,
The fresh coffee he offers warms her body. Sharing this salty
morning with him will warm her soul for months to come
'til the waves call her back,
alone again.

-- Linda Bearss

Bracklesham Sands – 1965

After the painting by Rodney Burn

the name is close to brackish and seems to fit
its bland ordinariness on a colourless day
where the tide is out and has been for a while –
long enough for people to pitch a deck chair
gather to scatter at intervals as punctuation
in the geometric curves where water has been
and sea shaped pebbles imitate the much larger
rounded sweeps –
                      the sea is a slit in the distance
from here a constant hiss in the breeze
all this beneath a light but flat uneasy sky where
the vastness of shore and heavens demand
we ask for superlatives of language to describe
figures in shirtsleeves-turned up trousers-sunhats-
bathing costumes and towels are just so apposite

-- James Bell

Surfers

A glint of wetsuits
scythes the Langland surf
on a roller day,
waxed boards
fizz the siren
of lathery spray,
a witness of blue sky
above the winter-music
on a morning balanced
for a marine rodeo;
the sea-dog
emperor of the bay
with thumb erect,
nature's surveyor
moving like a maelstrom
towards the fluctuating shore,
a reflex of surfers,
the energetic insects
on the skin of Neptune's
melted rink.

-- Byron Beynon

Seaweed

Feathery ceranium, sea grass, oarweeds,
a family of names holdfast
on rocks and in pools
washed clean listening
to fragile songs echoing
from the drowned;
hypnotic, light movers, weeds of red,
green and brown, sea lettuce,
the channelled, serrated, knotted,
bladder wracks, cladophora,
choudras, rhodymenia, laverweed, corallina,
black hair of the ocean, touch of softened
fronds, a tender sway and natural swell,
a symphony of leathery fashion
with the brackish sound of words
beneath the slanted soft rain.

-- Byron Beynon

Cefn Sidan

Before the arrival of places and the breaking of silences
I knew these elusive dunes and sea,
a wonder of landscape soft-running
as my hour-glass of childhood met the laughing air;
a myriad grains each with a history,
razor shells, jellyfish, footprints,
all become one in that tunnelled memory
where time is a perpetual summer.
The gulls within their portrait of coastline
sense the familiar ebb and flow
as a magnet of sun
propels their day across sky and shore.
The cartography of then,
indisputable and true
the white foam surviving
with the burning salt in my hair.

-- Byron Beynon

Wanting It All

For Evan

I want to worship the beach.
I want to dig for gold
and ancient stones.

I want the sun to shine
before it shuts up
for the day.

I want to swim far out
and talk to the whales,
touch their soft skin,
rubbery & sleepy.

I want to be a deep sea diver
and discover the sunken ships
last seen in books
and movies.

I want taffy and lemonade
all day and sleep on the sand
while moon comes up
from the blue-dark water.

I want to take the beach
back home and keep
it warm all winter

like a pet
like a bowl of soup

from an endless
pot.

-- Doug Bolling

Going To China

Time of the beach.
Time of your life.
High winds sweeping in
off a gray-blue sea.

Jolted tents tilting
like tired rubber bands.
Bad hair days everywhere.

Out there whales, sharks
sunken boats in rusty bright
nobody sees.

Maybe sailors' bones
from pirate days,
gold sinking into ocean
floor like moon behind
the mountains.

And we in our five year old
fantasy trip.

Sand castles, hide-and-seek
in the dunes,
grownups asleep in their
wrinkles of bad flesh,
mouths sagging,
bellies bulging
from all that grease
and beer.

But this hole we're digging
faster and faster,
straight on to
China.

Yes China.
Land of the other
side, mystery
hanging from
silver trees
like wondrous
ghosts.

We knew the tale:
dig down for enough
and you'll
be there
in all that
glory.

Our toy shovels and buckets,
hands scratched,
blood of heroes.

Until the gray haired
gentleman stopped to
survey the next generation
hard at work.

You kids better watch out
he says peering down
into our tunnel of love.

If you get there and
the ocean lifts up,
your hole will drown
the whole land
of China.

Then what would you do.
They'd put all of you
in jail.
You'd never get out.

They'd stick you with pins
and feed you to the snakes.
Keep digging. Keep digging.

He spoke. We heard.

His giant steps as he
wobbled off into the sun.

We were scared to our bones.
We were blooms of guilt.

One of us said:
we better fill it up.
We better get out of here.

We were gone.

-- Doug Bolling

I Want Him Not

She floats.
Currents carry her
tides rock her back
and forth, an infant
in a cradle she floats
moonlight shimmers
fog banks quiver
mists sculpt memories
and she floats.

Journey stopped.
Sky above, studded strangers
no north star (that she remembers!)
no orion's belt or pleiades
no dippers, big or small
no milky way.

Webbed fingers
outstretched, salty tears, soul
keening she plucks
pods from a strand
of kelp.

I want him.
I want him not.
I want him.
I want him not

Stars blink out
dawn surfaces.
She draws up her hair
like an anchor
disembarks from
this murky dream decision
finally made.

One last glimpse of the
sandy shore
flashing turquoise
and silver (a
silent
splash)
forsaking her mortal man
she escapes to her mother-of-pearl
caverns adorned only by her fluke
of many colors.

-- Nancy Brashear

What the Sea Gives Back

long before there were Wednesdays and Thursdays
before the voice of the lawnmower was heard in the land
there were long nights of starlight
sunlight filling the tide pools
creatures swarming and dying
waves washing the shore

it's still the same
the tides, the stars
the song of wind and waves

only now you can walk along the beach
and find a lightbulb covered in barnacles
fragments of bottles made smooth and mysterious
and a green molded plastic toy soldier
aiming his rifle
barely changed by the sea

-- Bob Brill

Beach Sonata

Starry night on a deserted beach.
No one there to see
a meteor flash across the sky
or hear the incessant murmur of the waves.

Fingers of ocean
caress the ankles
of a forgotten beach chair.
Wind riffles the pages
of a book.

Dawn light.
Pearl gray waves roll up the beach
to sink into pearl gray sand
and slide back into the sea.

The beach chair lies on its side.
The sea has swallowed the book
and spit it out again
to lie with the other detritus
left along the high tide line.

As the sun climbs into the sky,
turning the gray waves green,
the sand a brilliant white,
an elderly woman walks the shore
stooping to pick up shells
to send to her grandchildren.

By noon
umbrellas as far as the eye can see.
Nearly naked bathers jammed together
like factory farm pigs.
Women's bathing caps dotting the seascape.
Body surfing youngsters
scraping their bellies on the sand.

Young men diving head first
into the oncoming waves,
when they're not trying to pick up girls.

After the sun goes down
the families depart.
Time for the lovers
to grapple in the sand
still warm from the sun.

One by one the stars emerge.
When the sand grows cold
and even the lovers have gone,
the beach returns to its primordial state,
except for the lost flip flops,
toys and towels,
abandoned drink cans and condoms,
and the lifeguard's proud imperial throne,
fading in the dark.

Another starry night.
No one to interfere
with the perfect solitude
till dawn and the umbrellas return.

-- Bob Brill

The Season of Tropical Irregularities

the blue eye opening in the sky,
a graying, a washing of seed,
a great ray slips into the shallows
and warm waters form shadows
around him. In the distance
the eye blinks and sunshine fills us.
We light the bonfires and pass out
sticks, marshmallows, graham crackers.
Soon the eye will blink again
and we will leave the surf and sand.
This storm is an easy one, the trees
bend to the wind, and we make
our way home to plywood and shelter.

-- Michael H. Brownstein

At Cavelossim

Thirteen years old, Renuka
walks miles of hot sand,
in a bright cotton sari.

Bagsful of knickknacks
drag her shoulders down;
but she smiles at every tourist
and knows whether to say,
"Hello" or "Guten Tag."

One day, she stops
to rest, build a sandcastle
and practice English:
*cooking-room; sleeping-room,
chickens, garden; our own well.*

She skips off to find gulls' feathers
to stand for coconut palms,
and stones to mark out fences

-- Lesley Burt

Do Not Drown

dip foot
tread sand
tiptoe deeper
shiver until
water hits
solar plexus
gasp
flounder
wave

-- Lesley Burt

Resenting Dead Fish

Decaying faces stare with
glazed eyes and open mouths;

even the ducks
spurn the smorgasbord

strewn along the beach
in a random pattern of death;

who knows what happened –
perhaps the gods were angry;

who cares –
not the boys who found twigs

and hooked the fish in their crooks
flinging limp bodies

back into the water
to see who could make

the biggest splash.
Fish die – they aren't immortal,

then again neither are we –
most adults resent the reminder.

-- Fern G.Z. Carr

Afterlife

On the beach, a little girl's gold shoes
fill with wind-blown sand.

She left them behind as the ocean leaves
shells at the tide's edge – lightning

whelks, scallops, clams – to remind us
that what once lived inside is gone,

that our bodies, like shells
like shoes, will be emptied, filled

with wind, with earth, with light
as we walk barefoot into night.

-- Beth Copeland

I Need Your Beach

sand licking my toes
a kiss of sea breeze washing
over the shores of me
rocks of a distant island colony
secluded and alone
brackish barnacles washed onto
the shore; heated sunlit pools
dancing joy into my wearied bones
this is where i long to be –
ebbing here is no good for me
i am not an ocean there is no guarantee
that i'll flow again beneath the joy of
sun star gold, this beach has too many rocks
eroding into the sea there is no soft sand
to kiss me with a summer salve of
laughter and comfort; there is only the
crushing weight of lonely country roads and
trees with all their wisdom hanging
whispers of entropy over me –
seashells of doubt and starfish of despair
barnacles broken and brash screeching
insults i long not to hear; sand dollars are the
only currency hanging to my threadbare pockets
poor and broken, feet bleeding i'd be devoured by
sharks if i entered the sea but without you i'd
rather be torn into every piece of stardust that breathed
live into my veins than to remain here on this bitter shore of
wolves, bears, and crocodiles all eyes me with fangs
rife with the sharpest entropy i've ever known.

-- Linda M. Crate

Bricks on the Beach

ochre litters beige,
has been rolled like dough for years,
leavened by the illusion
of heat.

yet the scatters speak of crash,
bits of gemstone left over
when profit-making facets
caved.

ingots of crushed idols.
splinters of clay mansions.
eremites.
solidified tears.

a see-thru crab
fat as a silver dollar
ambles over stubs
once tall and picturesque.

the sea flogs them
with bladderwrack.
a pillory of gulls
swoops to berate.

only one rectangle left
in the plateau of the broken,
half lost to anonymous sands,

quiet as a dingy going under
or a grave without writing
on a rusty bed.

-- Chris Crittenden

Sun Beach, Vieques

for Lee

Like horses that roam here, unbridled,
the woman with a wind-swept mane

walks the crescent beach at dawn.
Daydreaming, she rides, pulse on pulse,

flesh on flesh – perfection dashed
when an aged mare drops

a stillborn foal before her eyes.
She wishes it snug in her arms, but

two boys take hold of tiny hooves
and heave the carcass out to sea.

Another day she spies a flash
of red half-bedded in the sand –

the saddle girds a pony torn
from a carousel by an ocean gale.

She strokes the thigh and sculpted mane,
brings new life to walnut grain.

-- Betsey Cullen

Santa Monica Pier

It leads me out into the ocean
suspended between the wave
and air
between now and when
I was a child.

Grandparents pass by
patiently holding their children's children's hands
pausing to point out
the waves pouncing upon the jetty
lions on the attack
charge forward,
race back
roaring beneath the boards.

Red, yellow, blue,
the lights blink their welcome to me,
the pier is filled with the incense of French fries
and cotton candy,
the old boards are full of motion:
the pinball slap shot,
the video game shoot down,
the merriest go round and round,
trying to steal a careless hot dog
and below
the waves testing the pilings, then breaking to the shore.
The ceaseless same drumbeat of tides going in,
time passing by.

Here I stand by the railing,
suspended over the question:
does time wash everything away?
But the barker begs me to take one more chance
so I will turn back to the jingling arcade,
the wheel is turning

so put your money down,
a winner is born every minute.

>   *-- Oliver Cutshaw*

July, 07

July, in white-hot nakedness
The moon, burnished orange
Bounces along the sands
In three quarter time
The clouds thick as afternoons
And sunsets like spilled wine
Across summer skies

July, when vines scale barn walls
And head for the clouds
When passing moments
Smell like clover and new mown hay

July, full and bountiful
Even as a thin thread of autumn
Is dropped to dangle _____
Into tomorrows' misty dawns

-- Susan Dale

Comes Time

Blue seams of the heavens severed
Rages of an eternal Sea
And the stars' wild screams
Blazing through skies

Glaciers rolling through time
Boulders splintering terrains
Wind shouting storms
Winds humming tranquil verses of rain
The clay molded from dreams
Awakened to hungry souls with empty arms
And hearts held in bone-stone loneness

From burning hearts came
Rings of fire that encircled man
And his daughters walking barefoot paths
Beneath the many faces
Of the sun

After false springs and empty darkness
Came a flash of dawn
And a child who waited under the rain

Came a slow measure of the moon
Throats of song
Plumes of goddess clouds
Sprouting pistils of yearning

Came sunrise molded in delicate tracings
To warm a seaside holding
The thin sands of time

Came the arteries of a river
Clothed in mist
And a larva of longing
That hung on to hope

Through bitter winters and precarious springs
Came comets and restless seraphim
Came the summer ferias we followed
To the crossroads
Of turmoil to life

-- Susan Dale

Solstice

I know the summer solstice.
Gray on the horizon threatens
an argument. Then rain

tropical, steamy as sex,
as if the sea moved inland,
streets knee deep until the sun

remembers, emerges, wipes sand
from cloudy eyes, turns emerald
each tear on each leaf,

exhales slowly and caresses the air
with the scent of storm washed grass.

-- Jessica de Koninck

This Boardwalk Life

(Bruce Springsteen, 4th of July, Asbury Park)

The storm heads dead on
for the Jersey shore
Of course she does
She is named Sandy
If you don't
know the words
you should not be here

-- Jessica de Koninck

Peaking

You, child of asphalt and street lamps, abandon
your city feet, embrace the burn of sand
and descend to the line where tan
turns gray, hot turns cool and wet.
You will find something here,
something unbridled
that your city cannot
offer no matter how
many miles you
walk. Let the sea
spray make your skin
sticky, your hair curly, your
skin freckled. Plunge your soft
hands into the surf each time you
see a glimmer of glass; present each
shard to your mother, beaming. She
will be proud. Wet sand thrown like
snowballs reconciles any disputes
you may have with your siblings;
it makes a satisfying splat but
does not hurt. You will fall,
gasp for air as waves toss
you about like laundry,
and you will resurface
laughing, hair leaking
seawater and sand,
sputtering from the salt
on your tongue, and you will
remember this, even when the tide goes out.

-- Hannah Dellabella

Nature in a Crowded State

this gray-green ocean is not
a postcard but it is
mine. between the gaudy
carnival of Casino Pier
and the sea-battered jetty.
the people bask in their pride,
this great tradition of summer
down the shore. they do not want
for aquamarine waters, sun-jeweled
and tepid against clean,
bright sand. our Atlantic bites,
cold teeth that turn your body
to pins, needles, and blue lips.
this coastline is not serene;
the roaring voice of the ocean
mingles with peopled sounds:
the shrieks of girls splashed
by mischievous boys, lifeguards'
shrill whistles taming the masses,
the laughter of siblings racing
from water to sand on the crest
of a breaking wave. this coast
is no tropical paradise but
it is nature for New Jerseyans
escaping the manicured suburbs
and gray smog cities crowded
by some nine million people.
our Jersey Shore is not
some television fad, some piece
of "dirty Jersey;" it is our summertimes,
our traditions, our remnants of nature.

-- Hannah Dellabella

Without Thread, Here, We are Connected to Everything

These are good questions to bring to the undertow,
the shadowy silt that can muscle us deeper into the tide,
past where the tide becomes manageable, past where
the steam of the ocean peters out on the sand in a near
ecstatic teasing. These are good questions we ask the dry
sand as it becomes wet sand, holds its breath under water
for long portions of the day. These are good questions
to whisper into the reeds, where the small children's arms
become too tired to bring their large shells up the wooden
stairs to the vacation home or the vacation motel across
the street from stucco condominiums. These are good
questions to ask while refusing to look at the moon, the draw
of the scene, the curtain and the pulleys of it, and as we
concentrate mostly on the passing of time, we have other,
more important questions about our own bodies, about
the wonderful feeling of being dirty in water and never
knowing what part will remain with you underneath the low
flow of a beach shower. These are good questions, the small
queries we have about our own imprint, shrank to actual size
next to the tremendous sea, about our relevance and lack
of hold on the rope that rolls the entirety of what has brought
us here in the first place. We have questions, many questions,
and with such a context laid out in front of us, we have no choice
but to believe it matters most of all that we ask them out loud.
These are good questions, the empty shells, cracking underneath
our toes are simply a beautiful distraction from the pressure
of the sun, which has seamlessly take the place of the moon.

-- Darren C. Demaree

September

lifeguard chair
empty
wind-whipped waves
lapping on the shore
reclaim their beach

-- Laura Dennis

After Crabbing

*"The innocent feature in babies is the
weakness of their frames; the minds of
children are far from innocent."*
                        -- St. Augustine

Blue shells teem in the bathtub, drag escapees
down again. The roiling mass flashes black

under dim yellow lights. In the kitchen,
all four burners lap the dented crab pot.

In pineapple hair ties and SpongeBob sundress,
our daughter roves from tub to stove, ferrying crabs

to the pot. She climbs the stepstool, watches red
signal death's other shore, and skips back for more.

                 -- Andrea Janelle Dickens

Hatteras Evacuation

Today's breath felt tropical, morning rising,
a taste of something foreign in the wind's
accent.   Bands prowl like animals, slink across
a clear blue sky. The light shimmers and sparks,
shifts and fades. Side by side, fear trails,
                              centrifugal.
We wait for the litany's next name to be called.
I will remember to trail my left hand against
the walls of every new maze. The sand knows
the fear of being lost
                    far away from home.
It hunkers down, for all the good it does.

***

In the daily offerings of abandoned periwinkle
shells, sea glass and driftwood, the summer
slows to a stop. Labor Day restless,
the broomsedge nods to us.
                    At home, a comet-track
scratched on a weatherman's cave wall
flickers on the snowy television. No prophet,
no prophecies.
          The sea's belly barely rises
while it holds its breath, and the searocket aches into
blooms fuller than yesterday.
                    *Beauty is the mouth
of the labyrinth*, Simone Weil said, *and at the center
is God waiting to eat us up.*
                    Or if not us, our house,
our sand. God tucked in a storm big enough
to dissolve all Hatteras back to creation's
                              second day.

***

Anticipation carries the worst weight, heavier
than sandbags at 2am,
                           squeezes us tighter
than the Tetris of dog crates, suitcases,
a child's car seat.
                Beyond the crepe myrtle,
our neighbors toil in their separate bolgia.
Like inmates, they bob and dive, dive
and bob.
         As if Dante made them hammer
boards across windows for all eternity.

                ***

               We wander in order to stay.
                         The lines of cars
         our own dust-and-ice comet tail across
         the sound.

That's all any of us can do, our backs watching
                the tangles locks of some heretic, whose name
                we whisper like a curse, as she emerges
                from the horizon.
                The sunlight will shift
by the time we're across the sound,
falsely hail us with sharp-slanted rays, mocking
some Renaissance Annunciation.

                ***

The palms have begun to hail our cowed
exeunt omnes.
              Heron fled inland before us,
dusk-colored paracletes, their coarse croaks
mock of our own warbled displacement.
                                Cowed,
no one reaches for the hems of fleeing saints
who seek quiet retreat from crowds.

                              We're waiting
for a sign that no prophet will arrive in town
this week. No temple veil shall be rent.

                -- Andrea Janelle Dickens

Sargasso

My feet cast for sandy patches between seaweed
tessellations, windblown and wavetossed, between

sea glass and coral fragments. Among the leafy
rubble green sargasso bladders, little watery

globes contain an entire teeming universe, souvenirs
of their travel. Unseen turtles raise their young beneath

the vines still floating out at sea, their safe nursery. We,
too are sargasso in our own right for others we may

never see. Beauty can only live in shadows where
the blinding glint is gone. Beauty enchants and

seduces. It covers us like seaweed. And we shelter
among it, bound like unsuspecting skiffs. Our watery

heavens are pierced with arrows of its brown and gold.
The leaves lay jackknifed across the beach, wrecks of wrack.

-- Andrea Janelle Dickens

Sand, My Old Friend

Ian wiggled his toes in the sand for the first time this summer season. It felt good and to his relief it felt normal. Last fall Hurricane Sandy had ripped up the boardwalk. He and his Boy Scout troop had spent the first few weeks helping to distribute food and water at the baseball field. In the following months they helped with storm debris cleanup. A few weeks ago he had stood on this very beach and wearing rubber gloves that were too big for him he picked up trash. One of the items he found was a waterlogged teddy bear. He put the bear to the side and brought it home with him that night.

He sat the bear on the edge of the beach blanket and thought of where it started out before washing up on the beach. Was he a prize from one of the boardwalk stands? Maybe he was a loved and cherished kid's toy. Had a little boy or girl been looking through the rubble of their destroyed home trying to find him? The sadness of the loss had stung him deeply. He had friends who had lost everything. He remembered the matter of fact way his friend's parents would say, "At least none of us were hurt." Ian knew better. How could you ever feel safe in your home knowing that nature could just suddenly wash it all away? His mind was brought back to the present when a little boy let out a loud shriek after running away from an incoming wave.

Ian smiled. Being in his early teens he could still appreciate the fun that being chased by a wave brought to a child. He walked closer to the water's edge carrying his boogie board and sat down in the sand. The water looked crisp and inviting. He looked back to his parents. His mother was setting up a beach blanket and his father was wrestling with the umbrella. He turned and took off his tee shirt. Looking into the water he thought of what else was out there. The image of the Seaside Rollercoaster stuck in his head. The huge metal rollercoaster sitting out at sea looking lost like a waterlogged teddy bear. He began to lose interest in going into the water. Maybe he would go walk the new boardwalk instead. Just then a little boy walked up to him holding a pail and shovel.

"Hi, my name is Timmy. Can up help me make a sand castle?"

Ian smiled again and shook his head yes. He knelt down next to Timmy as the castle took shape. As they worked Ian looked around at the homes along the beach. Most were in some stage of repair. Workmen were replacing all that had been taken away. Ian then looked to the ocean. He watched as the old sand was washed away and new sand washed up to take its place. Maybe that is the way things are supposed to be with the old making way for the new. Ian heard his parents laughing. His father was tickling his mother with a straw and she was trying to get some sun. He had been lucky. The storm hadn't affected his family that much.

"Hey Timmy, how would you like to learn how to ride a wave on a boogie board?"

Timmy's face lit up and he shook his head yes. Ian picked up his board and headed for the shallow water. He wiggled his toes as he walked.

-- Richard Dyer

Sheer As the Water Itself

Where the crowd clears a little, Olive comes to a stop. As she spreads out the blanket, her dad unfurls the umbrella and sticks the grip in the sand. "Sit under this, Jimmy, so you don't get burned like that man." The foundling's skin is whiter even than an O'Leahy's. Out of his clothes, his tiny body seems tinier still.

"But it's not raining," Jimmy observes.

Olive arranges the boy in the shade of the umbrella and takes off his hat. "You can have a bit of your cookie, but be careful to keep it away from the sand."

Several children scurry loudly by. "A muster of kids," the little boy sings, "a fleet, a flock, a posse, a pack."

"A nursery school on a field trip," says the old man.

"I was vaccinated at a school," says Jimmy.

Olive's dad points to the waves rolling in. "There are schools of fish out there. You'll be going to a school for kids next year."

The boy's future makes Olive as uneasy as his past. "Jimmy," she calls out. "Would you like to go into the water?"

"Oh yes," says the little boy.

"Then give me your cap," says Olive. "We'll leave it here on the blanket." Jimmy, stripped of so much already, doesn't want to part with any more. His cap—unlike any other—once lost could never be replaced. "If you wear it in the ocean, the waves will wash it away."

The boy takes it off, but holds it to his chest. "What if someone steals it?" Since Olive knit it, he only surrenders it when she washes his hair.

Now she ruffles his curls. "Jimmy, that cap is so much yours, no one else would touch it." What head but his would it fit? The boy beams but doesn't yet hand it over. "Here, we'll hide it under the blanket." And that's what they do.

The sea is not blue but gray and green except where it foams. Each new wave goes higher up the sand than the last. Olive and the boy, hand in hand, run to the water's edge and beyond. At first contact with the incoming swell, the boy squeals, and the old man, back at the blanket, swears he hears his daughter squeal along.

It's common now: whenever Olive's dad rises, the world around him ripples a little or a lot before smoothing itself out again. He makes his way to the water, gets wet, gets immediately cold and goes back to the blanket to watch. His daughter and Jimmy jump the waves as one.

Woman and boy tumble to the earth and let the murmuring surf wash over them. Sheer as the water itself, Olive has worn to a thin coating, Jimmy's protection, his second skin, his net, his anchor. Next to the fierce, feral attachment between them, mere love between mortals seems a flimsy thing.

On the way back to the blanket, Olive bends to pick up a tangle of beached seaweed. It's a kind of writing, but she'll no more readily crack its code than read barbed wire, a piece of lace or the foam the sea leaves on the beach, even after she closes her eyes and tries reading it again. Jimmy bends to pick up a shell, a pebble, another shell... Before he sits back down again, he hands the old man the riches he's rescued from sea and sand. One shell fans like a tiny webbed hand; another turns inward on itself. Follow the hole to the end and a man could get dizzy.

-- Jim Eigo

A Natural Event

i've seen walleyes dance
themes from the bottom
fins flashing
through the murk
swirling up sand
proudly showing
they never forgot
despite finding
concrete obstacles
to their mating beds
stoney-eyed fish
puffing bubbles
trying to get their freak on
met with cold walls

and scientists say
with regards to walleye:
"deterministic and stochastic events
may cause local extirpation
of populations with limited
opportunities for
re-establishment through natural events."

the long arm of the law
dips into the cloudy
Mississippi waters
and interferes even in
the walleye's bedroom
excuse us, we're having a natural event here

-- Will Falk

Divertimento for Sea and Sunscreen

Blathering airily on blankets rough with sand,
the sun- baked collective outwits heatstroke,
biding time beneath lotion, cabanas, and brims,
flouting the flagrant nerve of the rays,
rousing, at high tide, to yank the plastic
rakes, spades, buckets, and
sour-green molds of playful octopi
from the hurtling doom
of the cresting surf.

Early morning, on the empty beach,
there is always a lone red pail or yellow shovel,
half-buried at the shoreline, as if the
children, playing in primary colors,
were washed into a lather of foamy
grays and teals, as if there
really is no rescue from
inexorable tidal
loomings.

-- Kate Falvey

Sibling Rivalry

The Buick Electra winds through Topanga. Me & my sister,
we're in back. Left-tossed, right-tossed. Thrown together.
I'm in a two-piece. She's in a one-piece. We're halfway there,
& she has to pee. She always has to pee.

I can almost smell the beach.

Our lead-footed mama, racing up the canyon. Drives like a man,
she says. like it's something to be proud of.
Accelerate, she tells me, into the turns. Keep your foot
off the brake, both hands on the wheel.

I like boulders. I like rocks. I like looking at the canyon walls,
carved from granite, flake-away shale,
seashells embedded in the jagged cliffs,
even dinosaur bones, maybe, white, gleaming, jutting just out of reach.

Underwater, my daddy told me. Once, long ago,
the ocean rose up in a wet embrace. Tamed the earth.
Tore down the infrastructure. Rearranged the furniture.
Everything drowned, he said. Everything!

There goes Daddy, dashing off to work!
There goes Mommy, stepping on the gas!
There goes me, waltzing out to sea!

Crap in the trunk. Seaweed in the lunchbox.
We've forgotten the folding chairs.
Beachwood. Driftwood. The Continental Shift.

A leaf green beach towel spread out on the sand.
A long, skinny girl, spread out on the beach towel.

On smooth sand, snug between outcropped rocks.
A black ant licks my cheek. Watch your sister my mama says.
Like I'm the fucking nanny.

I swim out when nobody's looking. Lie on my back, rocked by the sea
A tuna fish floats by, doing the backstroke.
A dolphin floats by & winks at me.
Mr. Porter from kindergarten floats by, asking me if I've done my homework.
My daddy floats by, going somewhere else.

Back on shore, we find a jellyfish. Push it around with a stick.
Watch its ooze squirt out. It's poisonous! My sister shrieks.
I push it against her toes. It stings! It burns! She's such a baby.
Pee on it, a kid says. He takes out his penis, waves it around.
We laugh & dance while the piss-smell rises & the hot sun burns our skin.

My sister is crying. If my mama weren't calling,
I'd bury her face down in the sand.

-- Alexis Rhone Fancher

Sun and Sand . . . 'Flip Side'

And the stitches on your foot will be coming out when?
No, dear. High tide is NOT a police matter.
Yes, that fence belongs to snobs. Not to elites, like us.
No, don't touch that shriveled thing. It caused you.
Don't take mom's 'piña colada.' It comes with a free cabana boy.
Mom's SPF 999 didn't work. The high-end dermatologist is next.
No, those gulls didn't steal dad's checkbook. Read the above.
That is not a bird's egg. Rather a mother allig . . . OMG! RUN!

-- Elysabeth Fasland

Mining for China

They're digging deep for China
with plastic shovels and red pails,
their little bodies gray with wet beach sand.
So determined these tiny excavators,
but I look at my watch.
China must wait.
They dig like miniature steam shovels.
But my imperial mandate stands,
China must wait.
Five minutes more, please. No, just one. Please three.
Compromise. OK, two.
Mining rights thus negotiated and the time strictly monitored,
I settle in for at least a ten minute wait, I'm sure.
After all, China lies on the other side of the globe.
But no! These junior archeologists hold up their discovery!
Excited hands display their key to the underbelly of China,
a quart container with those exotic characters peering through
caked sand.
For them proof they've reached the magic land,
but for me the refuse of Lee's Third Street Chow Mein.
We all go home smiling and I'm half-convinced
both compromise and even faraway China
are sometimes reachable

-- Richard Fein

Before

we removed our strapless dresses
from bedroom closets
satin skirts tissue paper puffed
glass vanities covered by
cosmetic compacts
slid into gardenia bubble baths
that scented our homes
like Amazon jungles
this was the time in our lives
we danced
foxtrot mambo merengue
hips swaying
arms entwined
before JFK Cuba Dr. King
the Berlin Wall
dog days
before college started
and we waited with our parents
until the last minute
before the doorbell rang
for our dates
crew cut boys
who wore three button suits
narrow ties
talked about nothing
but power money muscle cars
took us to eat
at beach clubs
where we inhaled menthol cigarettes
through Audrey Hepburn holders
drank Singapore Slings Brandy Alexanders
Whiskey Sours
and afterward
beside low lit pools
on sun lounge slats
we explored each other's bodies

as the untouched moon
glazed the blue-black Atlantic
German U-Boats grazed
only sixteen years before

              -- Joan Fishbein

15 years later in Morro Bay

Soft grey horses try to bascule in the kelp,
foaming mouths wiped clean once more before the crest,
dragged down by washed up forests in the fog
the rhythmic patina canter all but dead

I look for ridicule or mischief in the her tilt,
some strange mistake, this carbon ticket paper's red,
too old, too cold, to stain my fingers, hot as ashes
on my tongue, began to blister as I said,

"But this says San Francisco to London in 98?"

She looks away, her elbows resting on the driftwood,
steepled fingers interlacing, squeeze the joints
above the polished nails lips bless her knuckles gently
and with whispered words my error she anoints,

"I would have come back with you."

And in the bay the gulls laugh loudly with the pebble
at the sound of fifteen years without her voice
when the wind whips up and gathers all the ponies
who gallop into shore to paw my choice.

-- Neil Flatman

Sand Surfing

"The sea stimulates words, and on
good days it seems its celebration
was made for us . . . "
                     -- *from Gabriel Mistral's "The Sea"*

Eyes closed, you and the sandpiper know
the peace where mind becomes ear,
thought becomes the roar of waves.

    The sea knows the shape of our music
    in the long curve of an oboe of driftwood
    waiting for a breath deep enough to stir it.

The sea knows durable styrofoam hearts
and plastic bottle top stomachs.
The frailty of human currency
in its broken sand dollars.

    The sea knows morning dew
    on tall spring grass through the sparkle
    of sea foam, in damp curves left
    on the beach when the tide pulls back,

the stripes of endangered tigers
and thriving zebras that race in herds
along the grassland – through its worn shells.

    The sea knows the colors of the desert –
    rattlesnake tan, bleach-boned white,
    and autumn sunset purple,

the texture of desert wind on rock –
smooth sandstone and pockmarked lava,
barkless wood and wave pitted glass.

The sea knows the brevity of a monarch
butterfly's life by the fast moving shadows
of red-tailed hawks on the spirals
of heat off coastal hills.

    The sea knows we carry the weight
    of the world on our backs and time wears
    it sea glass smooth, until we drop
    our burden, let it shatter on a bluff.

The sea knows the evanescence
of our souls – sea foam bubbles left
behind on water-stained sand.

    The sea knows our hunger for God
    with the persistence of sand.
    It knows how to reflect the sky.

            -- Trina Gaynon

Pages of Instruction Go Unread

I don't know why I like beaches,
I never water skied, or did somersaults in the water,
or launched off anyone's shoulders.
Always, there were many docks with cracked red coolers and wet towels
and many bobbing rafts too far from me to swim.
When I was 17, my friend Dennis from work tried to teach me how to dive.
He held my hands up over my head,
he placed my palms outward, thumbs touching.
For him, I dove into dark water, tasted murk and muck,
dropped hard then made it to the surface, he didn't see me.
Later, a black water snake wiggled fast from the smoky green water,
someone said, "Did you see that?" I nodded.

On the beach in Whidbey, there is little sand,
pebbles and driftwood spill randomly.
Shiny burned logs, black and wild as brittle cactus, split and splay,
from bonfires nights ago.
Once, I would like to spend a cool aired night there,
zip up my jacket, put the hood up tight,
shove my feet into a sand hut,
watch the lights pop on in Bowman Bay,
and think about what I didn't know,
what I lost in so many hands
that shaped mine.

-- Katie Hopkins Gebler

Fire Bird

When I stopped getting the unsigned Christmas card every year, I knew your kidneys had finally given up on you—all that candy and cigarettes doing a slow dance with your diabetes.

But if you were to walk up the sidewalk right now, in those white slacks and blue shirt with that pack of Marlboros in your shirt pocket, smiling that grin, calling me "tall drink of water,"—I do believe I would just fall over in a slump and melt.

We were so good together that we were bad. With Glenn Miller on the DVD now and the coastline at my door, my mind wonders how much of a paradise this place would have been for us. Tucked away on a dead-end street, sloping green grass down to the bulkhead, leading to the seagulls, pelicans and salty waves.

The minute I say your name, you appear; wings spread, circling over a vast area of Sycamore Bay, and land on top of a lonely pier post, mere feet from the shore. Then you look right through my window, spread your wings again and swoop down, then up, showing off in all your Leo splendor. You swirl and sashay, dive, fly, land again. I think of my departed friend Sylvia—whose Virginia Slims gave her a premature ride on the Emphysema Special—and wonder if you've met her. Notorious vamp, I'm sure she's using her charm on you. In a flash, you soar out of the majestic bird body and twirl away.

> *Zero in on her, fly toward her house. She is decades past 21 now and she's spent a lifetime thinking about you. When you first saw her, you flipped. You pursued her with a mad vigorous intensity because she was something else. You tried to warn her, but not really hard enough .You told her lies that she believed—for a while. But even when she discovered the truth, she stayed. It was too late. She stayed. "We won't talk about my wife*

and kids—ever. I won't leave them, but I won't stop loving you either." She stayed.

July 4, 1966. You said to always remember this date. It was a weekend of love making, dancing, scotch, coffee, Gran Marnier, 33-1/3 LPs and constant rain. But the rain stopped right at nightfall. I said I would think of you every July 4th for the rest of my life.

I often wonder if your wife is alive, what she's like, did she know about me—ever? Did you ever tell her? Did she care?

So, I try not to play Glenn Miller to avoid seeing you and your Leo wingspan where you transform back into the love of my life in white slacks and blue shirt, smiling, signaling, watching me—reassuring me that I'm right where I'm supposed to be with my rock-solid, salt-of-the-earth, trustworthy life partner.

I walk out to the beach where you linger a while until you are just a pelican, flying away, returning only when I invite you through music, a thought, a bright flash—like fireworks on the Fourth of July.

-- Sue Mayfield Geiger

Fragments

It's difficult to walk
       in this hot sand. My sandals
  slip. My feet burn,

      like the fever that raged
in my son's body after chemo.
    We turned down the thermostat,
        covered him with wet towels,
  could not quench the flames.

I just gave away the old recliner
      that bore his imprint but his
  grey robe still hangs
in my closet.

And here, along the weathered fence,
    a pair of flip flops, a faded
      blue towel.

                -- Patricia L. Goodman

Where Gods Encircle And Sins Recite

She speaks to white sands
unfettered by the moon's
sweet inflections of love,
those dark confessions blown
of blood and vine that spell
the pieties of a lover's touch
over the shores caressed by
foam and wave.

Beneath the vortex of a spindrift's
gaze, she listens to the foghorns
beshroud wails that echo across
the harbor luring the living into a
spiritual wilderness where dolphins
arch the horizons and random
constellations peer innocently in
fascination.

The skies peel back obeying her call,
an osmosis of emptiness that illustrates
stillness in motion between the sweet
salt embalms of night streams that glide
down a lover's body in intimate cycles
of privacy and pleasure. There is sparse
yet sincere rebellion in the lightness
of her spirit,

as it burns in waves of fierce grimaces
dropped unwillingly by the recurrent
pull of moonlight, part destiny, part
uncalculated doom, an initiation into
the deep truths of knowledge that hold
the remnants of the expenditure of love
with faint and pallid indulgent swoons,
where gods encircle and sins recite.

Whales, cold and deep, shift liquid as
they come up for air amidst the eerie
reflections of star seas, jellyfish, clams
and octopi, floating as waves rise among
the wreckage of a raft. Beauty settles
between dead pieces of wood, between
the rolls of life that lap over deep waters
guarded by Yemaya, Goddess of the Sea.

-- Zélie Guérin

The Sandy Shoal

She lay upon the chill, drying, sand disheveled.
Tomorrow would have been her twenty first birthday
unadorned, except for the seaweed in her brassy blonde hair.
Tip-toeing across her blue gray cheek, a pink crab foraged,
unhindered, it dined on the whites of her eyes.
Only the sea and sand cradled her now.

-- Deborah Guzzi

Sea Food

The ocean lolls in the Chesapeake Bay, salted sweetly
as sweat on bronzed skin, rocking the weary.
Translucent jellyfish bob on boat disturbed waves
creating a heat induced coma like trance in bathers.

Small pleasure-crafts at anchor rock rhythmically.
The ocean, womb to all, accepts, caresses,
each frail human laving languid limbs.
Toes explore the softer sand outspread.

Suited, we wade into the depth, worried
by the wet tug of cloth, in what was meant to be
an au natural moment reveling in the sensuality of sea.

With the skill of the hunter, hungrily, we search,
our feet seeking hidden mollusks, our eyes searching
for rising stream of bubbles which mark their breath.
Soon the buckets filled, and on the shore pits are dug.
Seaweed is gathered, and clams are steamed for dinner.

-- Deborah Guzzi

Back the Way I Came

If we got to choose
The manner of our deaths – rather than
The fatality of our fellow man
I would go into the water,
      back the way I came

I love the water and its buoyancy,
I love the sensation of being submerged
The silky feel of water on skin – perhaps I am less evolved than others
Perhaps I'm still part fish – a not-so-little mermaid,
Loath to slay her love so

I would choose to go to slip off my rock to
The bottom of some clear secluded pool
On a warm sunlit day,
The water's not quite blood warm
My naked body would sink to the sands beneath, I would
Turn into the sea foam and kiss mankind goodbye,
A frothy embrace and go
Back the way I came.

My atoms will disperse through the water,
Stardust to stardust, fish will come and nuzzle off my humanity
I have no need of it any longer
Freed from the prison of existence

I will go back the way I came,
My choice this time
Cradled in the warmth of the fluid from which I came
Giving back the cities and forests of man
Forming my passage from being back to nonbeing,
Just the way I came.

          -- *Judy Hall*

The Intertidal Zone

Five years old and
Left, as always, to my own devices, I
Waded into the Atlantic and started
Splashing aimlessly in the surf

We lived a ten minute drive from Jones Beach, but
My mother, frightened of the water,
Was more likely to take us to the familiar Town
Pool, with clear waters and reclining chairs

The complexities of ocean swimming were
Antithetical to my understanding; I thought of the Town
Pool and how I could dive in and swim the
Length underwater, wiggling my arms and
Legs behind me, mermaid-like.

The ocean was unaware of my inexperience
And indifferent to my impetuosity or my fragile mortality.
I saw the Atlantic Ocean as the Town
Pool writ large with the
Added excitement of magnificent seashells
And the silky dirt of sand waiting to be formed
Into castles replete with moats and damsels in distress.

In the surf, I found a speckled shell in a swirl of
Browns and purples. It fit perfectly in my
Hand, so I examined it in the sunlight,
Peering into the purpling fold when the ocean
Snapped up and swept it away from me.

Furious, I dove after it, not knowing the
Dangers of the intertidal zone where the
Undertow has the force of a Mack truck
And the mindlessness of an asteroid

I was dragged for what seemed to be
Miles, the gritty floor of the ocean like sandpaper
On my skin, my nose filling with the thick Salt
Water. All I could see was a black swirl and I
Wondered fleetingly if this was
What Outer Space felt like?

Sure that I was dying and curious too
I gave up, and allowed myself to be
Taken when the sea spit me out, a
Rejected lover.

-- Judy Hall

Stars from North Manitou

Slender driftwood femur stabs the sand, marks our spot,
small rotating claim
just out of reach

lapping notes played *delicato*, hushed windward stage bathed
in blazing molten honey
sweet on halting tongues
throats burning with pleas cast like flat stones

that dance away and slice the waves,
drawing beads of cobalt blood
that gather overhead.

Words, only words to the spider
already hard at work at the forked pinnacle of driftwood
thrust high into the band of prey orbiting above the beach
tacking an elegant array of spot welds
wielding slender batons in concert
rendering a precise constellation,
the only mantle of stars that matter to her.

By morning she's gone
bare driftwood marker
casting a long shadow
toward South Manitou
and you, still asleep in
a fold of dune beneath
the stars concealed in
mornings runny yolk.

       -- Dave Hardin

A Bit of Summer in Winter

It's a beautiful day
to visit the Jersey shore.
I stand before a large, casement
window in a New York apartment
watching snowflakes fall
against a gray November sky.
Slowly, I uncap a bottle
of Coppertone suntan lotion
held beneath my nose.

At first, I see only my reflection
in the glass, but it soon fades.
And then, I see the beach with
blue sky as a backdrop for small airplanes
dragging advertising banners overhead.
Multicolored pennants atop the beach pavilion
snap with every gust of salty wind.
Teens play volleyball on the brown sand
as the Beach Boys sing *California Girls*
from loudspeakers.
I feel wet sand between my toes
and the heat of summer sunshine
as I settle in to watch the bathers.
Smell of French fries, hot dogs
and beer collide with the scent of the
ocean brought in by the east wind.
Children sit near the water's edge
building castles with plastic pails and shovels.
Men strut with bottles of beer
holding in their stomachs
as they pass women laying on beach towels.
Bikini clad city girls looking for trouble
wind their way among coolers,
sunbathers, and lawn chairs.
Old men huddle under beach umbrellas
playing cards, listening to the Yankees game.

After what feels like hours in the sun,
I hear Simon and Garfunkle sing
A Hazy Shade of Winter on
a distant transistor radio.
And I find myself looking at my
sunburned reflection in the window,
holding the recapped bottle,
watching the snow on thirty-fourth street.

-- William Ogden Haynes

Ocean Day

The humidity of the past month has subsided.
The blistering sun bakes the sand into a scorching fire walk.
Summer has officially begun with the opening of the ocean.
Yellow and red capped boys and girls bob up and down in the water.
Dark chocolate tanned lifeguards peering through over exaggerated binoculars.
Barely clad teenage girls provocatively tanning their bodies to a lighter shade of black,
Teenage boys strutting their stuff up and down the beach,
Scrawny muscles and limbs in public view.
A dermatologist's dream come true.

-- Damien Healy

My World

I traverse
a fish pond world
gone black
by deadly feet
of swimming children
that pee
and splash
in the water I breathe

-- William D. Hicks

Holy Ocean Sonata

The holy ocean
took my pulse,
returned to me
more mystery
than the day before,
left me clinging
to my beliefs
as if they were a levee
I had to rebuild.
The water
was blue with
charcoal smudges
and whitecaps
winking to my self-reliance,
the whole body
of churning water
seemed to know me,
reaching with tentacles,
open mouth waves
inviting me to join
the communion
with the holy ocean.

On the shore
I took my pulse,
the sand beneath me
shifting in ever-tightening circles,
heat from the sun
stinging my pink skin,
a reminder
of past days
spent on the promenade
my fingers curled with another.
The sand sings to me,
a siren leading me
to stay

until the tide is high,
until those fingers return
or the leviathan
swallows me whole.

The holy ocean
asks for pieces and parts
for its collection
but I am already scattered
in the sand,
buried like a
forgotten beach toy,
left behind
by voices
on the highway.

-- Christopher Hivner

Shifting

I would run forever
along the wet sand
if I knew
the water wouldn't
try to consume me,
if the beach
wouldn't fall away,
collapsing around my feet.
Each step I take
is a reminder
of the edge
I walk,
the line that separates
my world
from yours
and hers and his.
I could run forever
if I knew the line
wouldn't move
and pull me along with it.

-- Christopher Hivner

I Am a Bronze God

I have been roasted,
my meat a succulent brown.
Juices coat my skin
forming a glaze
that attracts seagulls
and sand fleas.
Mother sun
has done her job,
now I will do mine.
I am a bronze god,
worship me
as I pose
on the beach.
You can look
and touch,
I belong to the
combers, players, bathers and baskers.
I have been transformed
to an idol,
the gasps I gather for food,
the cries of horror
inflate my ego.
You don't have to run away,
I won't hurt you,
I can barely move.

-- Christopher Hivner

One More Summer at the Shore

The hatchback opens its maw,
like a whale sieving krill,
and swallows her school of boxes.

She leaves the seine,
avoids the traps,
follows the sea route.

Traffic, like reflection, clears
as concrete melds to asphalt
then to sand.

Windows come down.
Breeze enters,
the salt of ocean, tears, blood.

Against the blue cottage
a silhouette, slim as sea grass,
waves.

In Dad's kitchen
he makes coffee
with water from the bathroom.
"You've got to fix the kitchen sink," she says.
He smiles,
a reminder to make an appointment
for the broken tooth.
"Doesn't hurt," he says
looking feral but harmless,
like a Gummi shark.
"I'll make a list," she says
"of things you need to do."
Her pen glides across paper
like a seabird foraging shallows.

"Shall I make one for you?" Dad asks,
and calmly writes BE.

-- Liz Hufford

A Beach Stained Indigo

The bluffs in all their pristine cathedral-like wonder
call with a persistence that haunts me day and night
In that shadow time that is neither dreaming nor waking
I go there and crawl through the mud on a beach stained indigo

The stones of my childhood run black with blood and tears
An old willow trembles, weeps dead snakes and impossible dreams
and tiny lighted vessels set off from the shore with all the people
I have ever loved aboard, and waving under the light
of a sickly moon, a double corona'd moon so lopsided
I wonder if it's the moon at all and not just some imposter nailed
into the sky and in the time it takes to wonder this . . .

The tiny vessels drift so far out in the lake; I can't reach
them; now they are ablaze and all aboard are screaming –
I keep brushing at my face as if spider webs are blinding me
If I can just get free of them I will wake up and everyone will be
saved

-- S.E. Ingraham

Genesis

Each step crosses another threshold,
I walk on a snowy white beach where
jagged rocks break the surface of
a tranquil sea and my shadow divides
into two figures – one of reluctance,
resisting the other's determination
to conquer this far shore – face up-
turned, arms loose at my sides, hands
open – willing to embrace, even you.

-- M.J. Iuppa

Sirens

the cool change tries
too hard to thumb a ride

on the seventh wave
and fails

my free time less sticky
than the air

watching my someday wife
in her element

outlined against the feline sea
lapping and lounging

on the shores of
our crusty confidence

dismissive of me
suiting its own purposes

a playground built
not on my lukewarm rules

here I am
on the flat indifference

skimming stones from my world
across the surface of yours

-- Miguel Jacq

Sydney

the thick Coogee Beach air
is climbing back out
of my throat

I am a stranger in
this master/slave
 mirror

horn blare
cuts off
city circulation

sand grit
riding the red light
up my crotch

even the heat
seems to push in
as we wait in a line
devoid of thank yous

-- Miguel Jacq

While the Seashells Listen, I Think I Love You

Lost love letters
lost to the rolling blue sea
  of early morning seashells
  of late evening driftwood
whenever waves roll high upon sand dunes
or bring forth new sand at low tides recession,

whenever the sea rolls...
                        I think I love you.

Your memories echo in the seashells-
your love splashes back at me
on the rolling whitecaps
all day long
while at sea
and disappear each night
as the white foam washes
back out to sea.

Or just at home, on a shelf,
one seashell echoes-
I love you
a thousand echoes roll
I love you.

I'm a long way from the sea now,
will you listen for me-
while they wash in
and wash back out again?

The seashells roll.

                -- Michael Lee Johnson

In December

In December Miami sun
stands out on the southern
tip of Florida like a full-
blossomed orange,
wind torn sunshine eats away
at those Florida skies.

Spanish accents echo through
Caribbean Boulevard loud
like an old town crier
misplaced in a metro suburb.

Off the east coast 90 miles,
westward winds carry inward
the foreign sounds lifting off
Castro's larynx,
and the faint smell of an
old musty Cuban cigar
touches the sand and the shoreline.

-- Michael Lee Johnson

Lost in a Distant Harbor

Love,
once beside me

now

lost in a
distant harbor

calls out into the night
crawls back into the fog.

-- Michael Lee Johnson

Beach Scene

At the seaside, she says:
"Mum, are my thighs fat?"
Dad's pet name for her
is Miss Ribs.
Pale in a navy swimsuit
she wants to gulp
back down the worry
that swims in her mouth.

Amid the buckets,
Frisbees and lilos.
lurk sandwiches
like great-white fins
and lemonade ice-lollies
with a joke on the stick.

-- Caroline Jones

Summer in the City

There is nothing in my life now
that is remotely like the summers
of my childhood. The soft, sweet,
tanned, dolphin that I was, at home
in the salt and sand of the cold Atlantic ocean.
Diving under white foam breakers into the inky,
mussel shell, silent blue of
smoothed rocks, shells, sea glass,
driftwood, mica sparkling and me
glistening, floating, diving, twisting
the sun warming the uppermost layer
of me, the ocean, sand, and air, while
the deepest layers stayed frozen custard,
Creamsicle, snow cone,
frozen in time cold.

-- Judith J. Katz

Who Has Such Phenomena in His World

A pod of dolphins are swimming
just beyond the human side
of the ropes and seashore buoys.

Slick onyx black fins and tails glide
breaking the translucent evergreen
August Atlantic.

They swim in a perfect line
the curvature of spines
a miracle of streamlined motion.

On either side of the mother
the babies mimic her movements.

Mothers on the beach are drawn
to the edge of the ocean.
Stand ankle deep in the foamy shore
their babies magnetically pulled alongside.

Transfixed in the moment
no one takes a picture
the image is embossed
directly onto memory.

Tonight all of the babies
will float to sleep
freshly bathed between
crisp, clean, cool, cotton
sheets like dolphins
dreaming between
air and water.

-- Judith J. Katz

Green Sky at Night

1.

The rain is falling
hard and straight down
each rivulet
an individual message
I cannot decode.

I wander around the house:
living room, dining room, sun porch,
kitchen, bedroom, bath,
looking at the screens
of open windows
watching for the inevitable intrusion
of pooling water on wood
wet fabric on furniture

I am waiting for the aftermath
of a destruction
I am complicit
in creating
by not closing the windows
now: before the microscopic
mold spores begin clinging,
colonizing, covering every surface

2.

I am global warming
all by myself, melting
imperceptively where
I should have polar ice caps
growing permafrost over
portable spring-fed pools

This is what I look like
after the hurricane blows through
the tornado touches down
the trade winds reverse direction

There is too much to care for
on my small planet
and that I alone care
for it dry it off
fight the invasive decay
choose what to salvage
exhausts my jetties

3.

I am a rock
in a rock
on a rock
and the weather drips
on all three of us
wearing down edges
until my sharpness exists
in a hollow cavity
dangerously lined with crystals
deeply hidden inside like
a geode

even I am not sure
what is growing in there
what color it is
how it was formed
over the years
into something
semi-precious.

-- Judith J. Katz

Einstein at the Beach, 1945

Poised on a rock, his back towards the harbor, Einstein
in shorts and a polo shirt relaxes for the photographer.

My, what shapely legs he has and those sandals: open-toed
with a strap around his instep, a slight heel. Legs crossed,

he could be Lauren Bacall summoning Bogie for another cigarette.
He is grinning. Surely he doesn't know yet about Hiroshima and
Nagasaki

only what it's like to be revered and to rue his one great mistake.
I think of him every time I watch the strangely prescient *Fantasia*:

the Sorcerer's Apprentice attempting his Master's tricks:
homely buckets of water turned into a tsunami. Even if Einstein

could contain his theories, tie them up like a packet of letters
shoved to the topmost shelf in the laboratory, he couldn't.

With scientists, that's not how it works: ideas shared, enhanced,
qualified, amended, and once out there made more beautiful.

The beauty of his math, his equations, cast a spell on the rest of us
so we think Einstein a metaphor for genius. He grins at the
photographer,

enjoying himself this fine day, the war close to its end, relaxing
with friends.
Who can blame him? Who knows what burdens his mind bears,

what private hell makes his heart ache.

-- Claire Keyes

Kayaking the Sakonnet

This is what she remembers. Heat.
A river. Lugging the kayaks to the beach.
Pushing off. Herself paddling out

ahead of her husband, wanting it more
than he, that feeling of buoyancy.
This is what freedom feels like, she thinks.

She embraced it all, even the fisherman
calling her over to view six stripers
as long as his arm. He was a fool

but she liked him, liked his success, his need
to share it with her. Could he see
that she too was full of life?

Her husband had pulled away. She followed,
passing close to a jumble of rocks
where cormorants spread their wings to dry.

She smiled at the little black crucifixes.
Nothing in this world seemed only one thing
and not another. Witness the jelly fish

floating pink and blowsy as peonies. Yes,
there was a shoal with waves striking
against spiky rocks—something to avoid,

as her husband, the cautious one, warns.
A shoal is a shoal. Nasty to boats.
But she can't resist

dipping into its seaweed necklace,
a coppery mulch with a scent of drenched leather.
It follows them home.

-- Claire Keyes

After the Hurricane

Our ordinary town beach becomes Ocean, at home
with Titans, waves swelling and crashing, the roar of it,

the foam, the shrieks of children. As if the waves meant harm,
as if they could take you, rip your feet out from under you,

toss you in a heap on the sand. For sure, there's a foolhardy
gene in me, an ancestral marker that says *don't hold back*.

Is that you, *mi abuela materna*, thrilled to leave Spain
for the wild west coast of Ireland, those cold northern seas,

the handsome Irishman you married? Or your daughter
casting aside old world for new, at age fourteen taking on

the Atlantic.   I plunge past the ankle-tickling surf
to the more serious stuff, just me and some boys

horsing around in the rough. A wave twice my size
looms up and I dive inside the gritty swirl, popping up

a little dazed, swimmer no more, but combatant.
Wave after wave leaps toward us, each massive curl

swelling higher, so outrageous and powerful I'm drawn in
and under, flailing, but not fool enough to stay long,

bathing suit flushed with sand, hair plastered to my head
as I stagger onto the beach where sandpipers patrol

the wet sands and children ferry buckets of water
to fill the moats around their castles.

       -- Claire Keyes

A Sail

Far out in the distance, a sail
silhouetted against the bright moon's
disc, and every eye on shore alive

to its pale form, waiting for a signal
to begin a song or a prayer
or some other chant, a welcome

and a warning amid the waves
and stars. Salt in the air and clouds
of humming gnats, a thousand breaths.

What ship grows wings across the sea?
What drowned sailors have found
their way to this wall of rock and wood,

their sad eyes only holes behind which
yellow flame flickers and dances
as if a wind were rustling in their skulls

and their frozen mouths could bring
some news of swallows gathering or storms
at the darkest places of the suffering world?

-- Steve Klepetar

Adrift

An unburdened pearl adrift on the waves,
tossed to the sea and stripped of all wisdom.

Emotional jetsam now ebbs with the tide,
forever untethered from port.

An empty bauble that reeks of perfection
by betraying the grit in its heart.

Free from the protective shell of creation,
and imprisoned in a quest for identity.

On dolphin backs and turtle shells,
afloat upon whim without mercy.

Its sorrow rides the albatross cry,
then falls in a green flash to the horizon.

Sinking beneath the frothing waves.
Drowning in doubt and swirled in obscurity.

Time erodes luster under salted tears,
as purity fades in the sun.

A prized and unique jewel.
A brittle scrap of rubble.

A burdened pearl awash upon shore.
Spent, lost and depleted.

Born of sand and to sand it returns.
An irritant underfoot.
A disregarded thorn in the side.

Absolved of beauty.
Mired in irrelevance.
Muted by the roaring surf.

                -- Craig Kyzar

Those Mornings on the Beach

were like growing young one step at a time,
a little girl again
craning my neck for animals you saw in the clouds,
our feet sprinkled with salt and sand,
we never let the water cover our ankles
but I felt its cold
five years old in a blonde ponytail
your arms a barrier between me and dark, dark things,
couldn't have felt safer if I tried
and every time I think of way back when
I raise my eyes--
the horizon is a mirror, reflecting oceans,
and I still look for sharks in the sky

-- Kate LaDew

Terrestrial Illumination No. 545

As a child he sneaked a touch
Of an elephant's horn,
An elephant alienated in a zoo.

He rubbed his fingertip over the white spiraling solidity,
And felt he had brought the alienated distance near.
It felt as if he were touching solidified moonlight.

This sense of tactile wonder stayed concealed
In his corporeality and whispered love to him.

All the popular pleasures the people advertised with their voices
As worthwhile seemed only trivia and petty
Compared with the wonder and rapture
He felt when touching living ivory on an imprisoned elephant.

One rare day, alone on a Florida beach, he intensely
Watched the spiraling line of foam waves brought to shoreline,
He saw as the waves lost their whiteness, their crest,

The waves washed away the sand's surface layer, and unconcealed
The quasi-gobular white bodies of sand fleas.
The sand flea's wings were like ivory.

-- Duane Locke

Volare' 1955

*"Just as the shovels get lost by the sea,
so do the children like you and me."*
-- Mason Williams

California trailer parks, on vacation
freedom of camping by the riverbank;
a pool to swim in, the summer dead ahead
and the sky an anthem I could sing from,
opening the windows of our Buick Special,
crossing at the California border
ready for the fruit and vegetable check,
the road emptying to Redding motels.

The whole wide Pacific Ocean lies ahead
running on the beach, snapping towels,
ear to the ground for razor clams,
girls posing their racks on the driftwood,
mermaids with tails and Domenico Modugno
singing his flying song whle I
try to keep my hair combed.

Burning with the sun, breezy as palms
and cocoa oil, I cover every pore,
lie awake listening to Mr. Aker Bilk
and hum "The Stranger on the Shore"
vibrato of his clarinet coming from
the bell of my throat while a silhouette
calls me back to another shape-shifter.

A girl is waiting in her swimsuit
I would hold her in a theatre chair
slink my arm around the back of her seat.
I sleep for two in my overcrowded bed
with thoughts of loves who abandoned me,
and I am already dreaming of another
who I can only imagine on a shiny cover.

Already I have memorized her phone number,
there are children growing in our garden
like hydrangeas with curly heads,
the wind has promised me a place
to live "Beyond the Sea" of Bobby Darin
where my future goes round in vinyl
just waiting like a new 45 to drop
from the spindle onto the turntable.

-- Michael Magee

Solzhenitsyn at the Beach

Note: Alexander Solzhenitsyn
      Nobel Prize Winner (1918-2008)

I saw him yesterday
balding, pot-belly, mutton chops
lantern jaw.
When he pulled his pants down
a moth flew out.
He was wearing his
swimming suit
with a red star.

I asked him about his
afterlife.
"I'm happy. I go swimming
twice a day."
I told him Putin invaded Georgia.
"Why Georgia, why not Florida?
That's where they are always
screwing up democracy!"

The last time I saw him
he was doing the Australian crawl
out beyond the ropes
having a smoke
practicing his dolphin kick
leaving the buoys behind
training for the next Olympics.

                -- Michael Magee

On the Coast

Remembrance is our religion, deep
fried turkey, bare feet slapping sand, South
African wine, gardenias, the forever
you see when you look past the shrimp boats.

Some of us aren't looking for yesterday, knowing
we all hug one nucleus. Some of us don't stop
searching for reasons – a holiday, a birthday, cancer.
Some of us can say just because, know we don't
speak of the years before buffers and therapy, let go
of monsters we can't name, while some of us pretend them away
with accusations. Some of us are an island of envy, vow
weekly phone calls, and some of us blame others
when we can't connect. Some of us notice

the houses on the beach get larger. Some of us take out loans,
max out credit cards. Some of us feel hurt when we don't
know about layoffs. Some of us wonder why we didn't
ask, or whether we disappoint. Some of us save
all year. Some of us watch us get drunk, become too lax
around the children. Some of us feel vindicated.
Some of us are rubber bands pulled
too tight. Some of us hardly need
an excuse.

Some of us don't want it
to be over. Some of us are counting
the minutes. Some of us will bring
a puzzle. Some of us will talk
incessantly. Some of us will go
for a jog. Some of us will find less
taxing ways to hide. Some of us have
special needs; some call it indulgence.

Some of us will smile through the cutting
remarks on liberalism. Some of us will angrily

defend the war(s). Some of us will
change the subject. Some of us will steal
away for a cigarette. Some of us will smell
the evidence; some of us will forget
by morning. Some of us make promises
before we even arrive – just a glass
with dinner; some swear we'll quit
tomorrow. Some of us will reflect
on the fact that no one's missing (yet).

Some will wonder if anyone enjoys these things.
Some of us will wonder why we married
into a family like this. Some of our spouses won't
come. Some of us will wonder why.
Some of us will ruminate on our own
secret problems. Some of us will stay behind
to clean up; some will hurry off.
Some of us will drive away,
hoping we do this again
soon. Some of us will drive away.

-- Jacqueline Markowski

Places to Go and Places Not to Go

Where the ocean lets go of the sun
I will talk to God. If he answers
through sand, I will send a letter
to my mother. I will say
I know it is wrong to choose
anyone over your children, a sin,
but what would she care? Living
in boxes so dark that truth and trust
blur beyond recognition.

I will march to the end of this
island, eyes closed, wings and teeth
bared. I will teach my daughter
words like menses and compass.
Her language will build houses one day
for which she will be hungry.

I will not walk into that
dark water at dusk. I have swam there
skinny, unafraid. It teems with anonymous
life, waiting to devour the wingless,
mistrusting creatures of the earth.

I will not walk back through
southern jungles that lie behind me.
I will not leave salt to spare the stubborn
nature, tongues so willful and savage
they nurse lies into adulthood,
name islands after castaways.

-- Jacqueline Markowski

Three's

Kalama Park, Kihei, Maui

They come in three's, she says – these crushing waves
    carving shelves on miles of beach and lasting
        days too long. *Like death?* I ask, grown serious

beneath the dancing palms. *Remember*
    three boys killed on Hana's curves last year?
        And then your father, uncle, aunt . . . and there's . . .

Look! she interrupts my list. *The turquoise top . . .*
    red shorts . . . white paddleboard . . . near the lava point.
        I bet he wipes out when the next three hit.

I'd like to think that patterns hold somewhere,
    that certainties out-trump surprise. But swells
        rage out of sync this week and I'm skeptical.

How do we count the waves flat-lined between
    their crests and foam? Or crisscrossed by undertows?
        Or jetty-split before they gain their height?

How do we count? In parts? In wholes? *Watch him!*
    she drowns my thoughts. *He's holding on . . . that's eight . . .*
        nine . . . ten . . . ! We cheer him on to shore, surprised

by his paddle-thrust toward the sun-soaked sky
    like some triumphant god conquering
        the restive sea for the millionth time.

                -- *Carolyn Martin*

Across Graves of Sand

Across graves of sand,
bones of water,
is callous spring,
resurrection of the blind,
deformed by Gods
of unspeakable paths and
beaches.

Among pariah's of deserted
coasts, I am supreme.
Simple as death is the body
of shore, with
strangers of light and sound.

I open gates of colour, soul waves
of exceptional tides, on which
butterflies of music indecently shine.
The sand writhes like snakes of wind,
on carpet of countless rays.
In its mouth, juice of light, grains
of vision, bells of silent corruption.

-- Austin McCarron

Neptune's Coquette

My toes throb over
hard pebbles. Waters slip
over slim ankles. Should I stand
shivering or go swim?
Lose my footprint?

Off I run, falling over myself
a mug of salty cider. This
wave an insecure bed.
Seaweed pillow. Carried by
moon to an abyss.

The floor of my mansion is
not tidy. I shall have sponges
for lunch. Ride with seahorses
perhaps.

On the far shore, my gigantic lover
smiles, kisses of surf. We thread
soft waters while sunshine
dresses us in golden sequins.

-- Joan McNerney

Beach Tao

On the Rondeau Peninsula in Ontario,
I walk with Bashō
along Lake Erie's north shore –
smooth small stones,
dead snub-nosed minnow.
Mist transforms to earnest rain
with wind in the willows, a great sway.
Lo! He is at home with egrets.
And I, at his spirit's side,
pass over driftwood
into shallow dunes. Yes,
I too behold cinquefoil,
witness yellow's firm grip in sand.
Along access path #7, heading inland,
a Baltimore oriole dashes orange.
Wind-blown, rain-soaked, I bow to Bashō
and he flies off, scarlet tanager, a red throb,
universal, who vividly pronounces:
I may be heron.
I could be tern.
I would surely be, surely be.

-- Karla Linn Merrifield

The Truth of Florida's Living Beaches

for Blair and Dawn Witherington

Several day-glo orange, sale-rack t-shirts
    deep discounted, overlooked,
        spell out the seaside alert to tourists:
            Life is a beach . . .

where Death is waiting to happen.
    It is or may be:
        in shifting dunes you're buried alive
            by the sudden accretion of Aeolian sand.

Or you tumble headlong at your peril
    over a scarp; or you survive
        but succumb to Hurricane Zora,
            her abrupt erosional force.

You may be pulverized,
    into shell-hash gritty bits
        or atomized into a few
            more grains of idle detritus.

Spilling, plunging and surging waves
    never cease to slay
        and may carry the last remains of stars,
            jellies and slugs to your final shore.

Dead-man's fingers
    wash into the swash zone.
        Spongy coral? Or its namesake
            from your body? Some of both?

Beaches are lightning hotspots
    and you may be the tempest's fleshy rod.
        Life is red tides, rip tides, and yours
            may be the poison of stinging hydroids.

One way or another, the slogan is fulfilled:
   We shall be reclaimed by the ocean
      some sunny day of ultraviolet rays
         or blank, black night of storm's certain surge.

        -- Karla Linn Merrifield

Seeking Heaven: Why I Collect Seashells

My shell eye is
a centrifugal eye,
a shark snail's blue eye.
It reduces the shorescape
to the shape and shine of death,
the glittering swirl
of cold geometry and refraction
in the swash zone.

My shell eye curves
inward on itself;
it is the inner eye
of a lettered olive.
It curls a spiraling
message to the brain:
High tide is time to glisten.

My shell eye peers
as would the shattered whorl
of a lightning whelk,
the arc of an ark
bleached white,
the scallop's black scallop.

My shell eye is the keyhole
of sadness in a broken sand dollar;
my shell eye is the polished
fractured disk of a dosinia clam
that weeps a glossy tear.
My shell eye glazes over.

In the realm of the newly dead
at the wrack line
after winter's storms,
I cast my eyes
on the myriads at my feet,

my shell eye on the shadows,
looking for the glint of life
in the afterlife of the sea.

-- Karla Linn Merrifield

At the Seaside

A ship sails
from the shining shore;
shimmering sea waves spread
secrets and shells all around
on the sleeping sand;
the seagull's shout
soothes our sorrows
as we sit in the shifting shade
of a scampish sun,
wrapped in the stifling shroud
of sweetish sweat –
sensing our soul's solitude,
sipping the salty sap of the summer.

-- Claudia Messelodi

Mahdia Beach

The long open beach stretches
from solitude to isolation,
it seems to run parallel
to the horizon which is like
a dark blue underline below,
a perfectionist painter's sky,
that seems only a pebble throw away.

The gentle waltz of waves
caress the grey, gold sand
leaving in an irregular damp
darkness which disappears
almost instantly before being
refreshed again.

The only piece of beach furniture
along this Tunisian shore line
is an abandoned, perhaps marooned
tree from a far distant land.
Nature has created a driftwood
sculpture in this quarantine of peace
where one can meditate on different
shapes from various angles:

a pig, an eagle, a walrus . . .

-- Les Merton

Inverness

Mist passes quickly through the canyon below this house,
Where the far pine trees are full of mysterious dark spaces

On the eastern side of Drake's Bay the fog piles up on the hills
Over bright green patches of vineyard
And camel-colored August grasses

A heron cries suddenly across the landscape
As if in answer, a buzzard begins to circle . . .

-- John Miatech

How Things End

The ocean called you loud in '64
When our family drove to the Pacific Coast from our home in distant
Michigan
For years afterwards you talked about the ocean
I always felt part of you had been left behind, somewhere on the wild coast
Between California and Oregon

And now my brother Steve and I have brought your ashes back
Shaking them gently into a small rivulet
The bright water carries you across the beach toward the ocean,
Past two seagulls that stand like honor guards to salute your journey,
One on either side of the steam as you drift toward
The great water and the unknown

The things I learned from you
I have carried far . . . all the way to here:
How to sew on a button,
How to lick the spoon when making cookies
How to hold myself inside when dad would drink too much, then forgetting
How to let myself back out . . .

When I learned that you had died,
I planted tulips and daffodils in my garden, your favorite flowers,
Knowing that is exactly how
You would like to stay in touch

The white specks of bone that are all that is left of your visit here
Finally move from the stream into the sea

Where at least a part of you has been
Since the ocean spoke your name
And you were there to hear it

-- John Miatech

Place of Great Water

I have been on the long ride
Around your body,
And while I have seen into your clear waters,
It was impossible
To see all of your at once

Your waters are cold and deep, but not unwelcoming
The wind that blows across you is powerful
And it reminds us that you are a path that we tread on
Only with your permission

Someday, I will come back to listen to your secrets,
The ones the bears along your shores protect,
The ones the wolves sing about when the weather grows painful,
The secrets the Anishinaabe and Cree live by

I will climb your rocky shores,
Look out over the swells of your body,
Search the deep water of your heart . . .

I will come for your beauty
Gitche Gumee
And I will marry it
To all I know

I will tell my daughter;
"Here is where your blood came from,
And you must remember this
To know who you really are"

-- John Miatech

The Boats

Tallying the keep of the season
slipped in harnesses of wire mesh
the sleepers wake on widow walks
distant gulls cry speed shifting
across waters where the worn hulls
drift listlessly off months till winter
solo orange men march the dock
hauling the traps up cabled lines
empty of the sea now and harmless
the boys turn to nails and things
in need of repairing their neglect
while the lobsters sleep growing
deeper green in the weeded undersea
restless, slow clawed, a future boil
on days when the fog returns
and the boats head out to sea again

-- George Moore

Along the Beach

A path through star-sprouted dust
Led to seawall, foam; the well-spent wealth
Of long past lives.

The path reshaped fathom and weed;
Cut through furrows of cracked shell, sea-glazed glass;
Emerged from a dream's prow.

The pebbles spoke of brine, wings; a sun-shower.

Unbeknownst to passersby,
A child reveled in the plush of time's
Unbroken sigh; the mesh
Of sky and wave.

-- Joseph Murphy

The ocean water tickled and I burned
the afternoon in sand. For hours I wrote
nothing, as far as product is concerned,

while thoughtless glimmers, like the sea, returned,
then left me with a salty, sparkly coat.
The ocean water tickled and I burned

beneath the sun, and in the stillness, learned
it isn't paramount to stop and note
nothing, as far as product is concerned,

but to stop at all. How often have I yearned
to write a thing that you would want to quote?
The ocean water tickled and I burned

notion to vapor as the liquid churned
the sand – and me – as if to say: Devote
nothing, as far as product is concerned,

to expectation! Discipline's unlearned
at best, or automatic, like the rote!

The ocean water tickled and I burned
nothing, as far as product is concerned.

-- James B. Nicola

Siren's Call

The wind.
Sometimes, it sounds like her voice –
the rise and fall of a wave
as it rolls on the beach.

She calls, finds me here.
Though I stand deep in prairie grass,
where waves sway
dots of Indian Blanket wild flowers.

*Come let me drench you
in the brine of my breath.*

The crusty weight of her humidity
calls out to parched skin.

The hollow under my arms
grow damp in answer.
Salt stings in empty places.

Then – she sends her perfume – that
heady brew of seaweed and driftwood.

There! See the beat of her waves on the shore,
like an EKG
of my heart –
gush, gush.

My feet, on flatlands,
hundreds of miles away,
curl around, and beg to dig
into the heavy sand of
her flank.

Just once more – can I hear the song of her birds?
Watch them rise on the breeze –

follow their skinny beaks as they
soar, dip, and dive down?

Then just as I widen my arms to embrace her,
she steps away.

As the wave ends,
I hear it singing . . .

forgiveness.

-- Christine Nichols

Beach Religion

Yellow-footed snowy egrets
stand in clusters at the beach,
accepting with no hesitation

two great egret cousins
whose feet are black,
and us, the human population.

Sun is burning through
the morning haze.
We talk of Zen and life riparian,

how to cherish, not to cling.
Buddhist too, she calls herself
a hyphenated Unitarian.

-- George H. Northrup

Ram's Head Island: New Ears for New Music

Broad tireless sea,
always waving to the shore—
rock, pebble, sand.

Out of city mind,
this island off an island,
lemon lighted leaves.

On the terrace now,
waiting for lobster and fruit—
sacred summer sings.

The moment billows,
cascades gently down the hill,
swells across the bay.

Farsight to insight.
The knowing instant opens,
here to distant shore.

Dissolute this one,
like pine scent on mountain air
carried off just now.

-- George H. Northrup

Black Sand Beach

I've seen a black sand beach
stranger than any foreign world
where King Poseidon draped in seaweed
once walked upon the Earth –

a black sand beach where steel-colored waves
wash up to shining, ashen stones
nested beneath charcoal plateaus that break out
all over in lime green leaves.
Neon-banded spiders cling to webs
in nooks that fill with turquoise pools.

I wait on beach-clothed friends to take their photos.
I, beach-clothed, wait and take a photo too:

silver sea spray explodes
against the crags of volcanic cliffs
where King Poseidon draped in seaweed
once walked upon the Earth.

A woman comes up from the sea with skin
smeared in black pumice mud,
trailing footprints that quickly fill
with metallic influx of seawater.
She's not a mermaid, not an oceanid,
just a tourist who laughs and claws
the air like a sea monster with aviator-glasses eyes
as we photograph her with our phones,
and roll our eyes at the show.

-- Bret Norwood

Buried Treasure

I was seven
When the truth came out.
Only a little girl with fiery ringlets,
The envy of the sun,
So unlike my brother's inky hair.

I was digging in the sand for buried treasure –
Some long-lost secret obscured by time –
The seagulls squawked shrilly,
But I ignored them and the noise faded
Into the background.

The sand became darker the deeper I dug, wet and gritty.
The breeze carried the scent of salty ocean to me.
I could smell the sunscreen
That my mother had applied so generously
To my pale, freckled skin.
She warned me that unlike them, I burned easily.
But I didn't care about sunscreen or burning.
My focus was the beach, and the promise of discovery.

When I had asked my brother to help, he laughed.
He went to talk to a girl who was laying on the sand,
Uninterested in adventures and pirate's booty.
He was twice my age and rarely found my ideas worthwhile.

The wet sand began to accumulate under my nails.
My chin itched and I scratched it.
Suddenly my fingers touched something firm; I let out a delighted squeal.
My brother didn't take notice of me. He was busy laughing with the girl.
I didn't mind. I didn't want to share it with him.

The breeze blew my hair into my face. I couldn't see.
I pushed it back with my sand-laden fingers then resumed my excavation
While a particularly brazen bird waddled towards me.

It was a conch shell.
A treasure from the sea.

Carefully, I rinsed it in the ocean.
Then I listened to its rendition of ocean waves.
My very own musical shell to commemorate this family vacation.
Our first.
Running to the house I stumbled a few times,
My legs unfamiliar with exercise on this terrain.
They didn't hear me arrive at the patio door.
The breeze pulling the white gossamer window coverings outside, then in.

I froze in the doorway when I saw my mother crying.
Mothers don't cry, I thought. Children do.
My parents were arguing, another first.

"You're the one who agreed to an open adoption!" my father spat, pointing at her accusingly.
"I didn't think she would ask to meet her," my mother hissed, glaring at him.
I dropped my shell.
The thud startled them.
They looked terrified and guilty, "Oh honey . . . " she whimpered.
"You're covered in sand," my father added stupidly,
She motioned for me to come over, "Let's sit down and talk."
I didn't know what to say. Or what to think.
I picked up my shell and held it out to her,
"I found buried treasure."

-- Jennifer Ostromecki

Mirage

no trees no traffic just this ruler straight
interstate leading to a blue mountain
range floating beyond the far horizon

silver lakes evaporate at our approach
a sea ahead completely covering the road
retreats in the heat before we can arrive

deserted ancient ocean sand not even damp
as another oasis appears draws us never nearer
to ever distant mountains in the western sky

-- Carl Palmer

Fishing

An old man leans from the porch, fishing pole in hand. He casts. The spinner spills fine line over tufts of grass and weed. *The ocean breathes today, but will it spit?* He reels. The lure hops, skips, tangles through the green. Beyond the yard, a beach of sand borders the sea, but it is not his way to come down off the porch.

From inside, a woman's voice. *Must you go again? Will you not, for once, spend a day with us?* Lure bangs rail. Sunlight reflections splash the ceiling. Why this memory of voice? Why this intrusion? He lifts his gaze toward heaven. In the sky, birds battle over a morsel too small to matter.

A flash of white belly. The pole whips in and out of shadow, and the lure, shining blue against the great blue sky, comes crashing down. With it, a gull, a flapping, flailing bird. His fingers clutch, his wrist rolls, slowly at first, and then with more intent. The bird hops and flaps, falls and flaps, is dragged across the yard. The old man should release it, cut the line, but that is not in his power today, or ever.

Staccato squawks become the desperate pleas of children. A beak snaps, a mouth gasps for air. She must have filled the tub one bucket at a time, one child at a time... *and where was I?*

-- *Stephen V. Ramey*

Ocean

The scent is pungent, the pull, urgent:
life vests forgotten

we dive in, recklessly gliding from
obsidian cliffs into the abyss.

High astride swells and tides,
heads tipped back,

our tears of laughter mate with salty
balm; faces caress fringing

curls of wrack and anemone;
shimmering fish dart around in me, alarmed,

fins fibrillating the flood.
Deep into secret places they thrust silver lips,

illuminating filaments of lust where jellyfish
quiver, tentacles unfurled.

Unfettered we ride the riptide,
churned to the current's cusp –

and as we're tumbled and dumped,
my blank and scoured cup fills up

with the sea.
The seventh wave sets us free.

Then lulled, languid and serene
we float

and lie, like two damp beach towels
washed up on a shy headboard

and draped
to dry.

-- kerry rawlinson

Beach Tide Pool

I look in the mirror

of the beach tide pool
& point right there

in-between my eyes,
& smack in the middle of my forehead
in the same line Mom had. I'd tell her not

to frown; rub it & think it'd go away.
But since then I've learned
the line is muscle set –
not caused by upsets

yet it can be frozen straight again
with a shot of Botox
What do you think? I ask the rippling
water & it answers back:
You're not the Botox type.

Accept it, you look like Mom.

-- Nina Romano

Swimming

A white butterfly
Hovers over some seaweed
Then dives
Into my stomach
Flying loops
Like Madame Laroux
Plunging into the heart
Of her Tarot
Somersaulting me
With the word "lover" till
My mind, bends,
Dives deep into the surf
Resurfaces,
Does the crawl
Then breaststrokes
As my brain glides into my body
To still it,
Readying myself
To dive again and with a
Push off from the sandy bottom
Come up, arms above my head,
I thrust and heave my torso,
In a touch-toes-to-feet dive downward
My spirit humbles
Till my sunken mind
And treading soul
Bubbles, gurgles,
Kicks upward
Toward sun and salvation –
Once again
Splashing
As I cut the surface
Flipping onto my back,
Floating, floating
Nearing where the waves break,
Toward the spot on the beach

Where once,
Holding a terry robe,
He waited for me under
A red and white striped umbrella.

-- Nina Romano

Beach Therapy

Hermit crab offers
one-on-one counseling
to gulls, terns, and sandpipers

Payment in sand dollars only

> *-- Eva Schlesinger*

Beaches

A jingle of crashing waves.
A waggle of sand hill cranes.
A wave from lofty sail boats,
an ornery child, an edgy mom,
a bucket overflowing with crusty
sailor words that should be poured
into the castle moat near a dad on the
beach with a bird's eye view of a jiggle of
curves and a sunset, a burn, a satisfied grin,
a slip of the tongue, alone in his world,
on a beach with a tan, vacation conquest,
victory complete.

-- J.lynn Sheridan

Reading into summer

A morning drive along the waterfront,
a swift unpacking of her floral beach bag,
pink SPF 99, a Diet Coke, a mystery novel-
a crime of lies.

Summer breeds a stack of reads,
stale from last year, punishing
under the relentless heat of boy and girl,

him plus her plus some things
she never bargained for that aim to burn the
hundred yellowed pages of her own love story
of passion number nine.

An afternoon scorch and a mire of
zigzag tan lines, one thought fixes
in her mind—
she'll leave him,
take a travelling job and fade out
of his life leaving those aged pages
of troubles behind.

Easy as a breezy summer's day.

A slap of SPF 99, a slap at biting flies, spilling her
now warm Coke onto her crackled crimson thighs.

spraying it onto the black-walnut tanned man
at her side, sprawled on a U.S. flag beach towel,
blue Semper Fi cap balanced across his jowls,

he hisses in the heat,
digs his right heel into the sand,
in the divot where his left heel should be—
her spilled Coke, her shooed flies,
they gather 'round his stump,

she averts her eyes,
she'll leave him,
that's what she'll do,
a swift turn of the page,
and she disappears into
the mystery of passion-less lies.

-- J.lynn Sheridan

The Bar

On aerial planes
I turn,
silver heels slashing the wrist
of land before the ocean
and the sand.

My dear, your eyes are moons
as they watch me
dance and pivot.
Such an external change!
You must think me possessed, yet
it is not my demons
who make me dance.

    *

I offer you my hand, smiles
dripping from my fingers.
They close on air;
you step away,
shaking your head.

I stumble, but raise
my hands valiantly
to the stars, refusing to fall –
to fall.

I dress my pain
in the swelling gowns
of euphoria. All I want now
is to escape you
All I want
is to be free.

The wind murmurs brilliantly,
sadly. I turn from it,

salt-water flecks my cheek.
Ocean-tears,
not mine.

      *

The tide changes;
nothing you can say
will prevent it. Perhaps
if you had danced with me!

The moon recedes;
my bare feet
sink coldly
into the quickening sand.

      -- Tamara Simpson

Questioning Horsery

(Introduction to Grayson)

There were six million, three hundred fifty-two thousand, five hundred and eighty-three wavelets on her face this morning. She refused to be a victim of dawn tides, exalted in the event she was able to do so. Lying on the beach, body of sand, spirit air, mind spent and set aside, she fell into the waking side of a dream.

Three directions surrounding, vertical columns, fortresses of stone, up and through a lavender/pink firmament she stared. Eyes wide open, other than a hint of a smile wearing her lips, one might imagine her quite dead. Water tickling, gooseflesh wearing, the three-walled prison of her existence suited her fine. "How did I end up here?" The question threatened but she pushed it away. Stone mansion, earthen room, ocean door; she needed them all and nothing more.

Startled by thunder, the incredible percussion of earth quaking, she closed her eyes. Not long though, this respite; she opened them just a bit, peered down across her body supine. Two rosebud nipples erect, extant reminders of her humanness, her flesh, met her gaze and pleased her. "I am woman." She pushed the thought away.

They came to visit then, magnificent and marauding, a stallion and three mares, manes and tails flying, rays of eos filtering, slices of dawn-light instantaneous, erected, broken, furious, wide-eyed and alive. Her arms, goddess tentacles, feathers lifting, rose from her sides to receive them. Mud silt exploded from their hooves, dappled her white-flesh, excited to ecstasy her nether regions, filled her with white-heat fantastic, orgasmic.

Body arched, wings supporting, she welcomed the tide, water caressing, purging her pinto/appaloosa and leaving her ivory/white. The stallion's voice roared as he mounted the precipice, the armor of his limbs taut, aquiver, a s ingle gasping breath, and Grayson let it all

go. She watched the mares disappear into the clouds behind him and entertained the thought, considered her options, that she might just follow. But no, she smiled and pushed it all away.

-- Tom Sterner

Suddenly Sunday

He remembered little of that day, but he remembered that it had briefly stormed and also that the bathers looked like cave art—swipes of ruby and yellow and jade on a wide brown canvas. Primitive. Even the backside of the clouds, majestic though they were, had the look of judgment undulating toward a dark end. He had feared at that moment that the divorce with his wife would not be finalized and that the memory of it would always be an assault on his advanced sensibilities. It called for a drink. From a compartment in the boat's dashboard he fished out his binoculars and squinted for a sight of his ex-wife's large, pink body. That was July fourth, 2012, the first and last holiday with the kid.

"Bitch, I know you're out there," he now remembers saying to himself. No one had heard him. Out behind him on an intertube was their daughter, Azazel, floating and singing—*Row, row, row, your boat, life is but a dream—merrily, merrily, merrily, merrily*—troubling his own drunken voice like the smack of the waves on the side of the boat. He raised his Vodka bottle and scowled at the beach thinking *burn to nothing, you sow*, as he throttled up the jet-boat and shot (like a ball from a Roman candle) red and roaring through the surf. His daughter waved and silently whooped, the after-spray a rainbow skewing out and down into her sun-burned face as they screamed past graceful sailboats and wind-whipped families clogging the center of the lake. He veered hard to the left and slung the kid out tense on the rope—a slingshot stone—the boat's uppity prow pointed toward the dam. Out loud he asked: "Got time for me now, Counselor?"

The next and inexorable memory was of his kneeling down over his daughter on the trodden ground of the dam; she was laid out in vivid color: red, white and blue—that much he could remember. Around her body a ring of oily sunbathers held themselves together with slick hands and wept. It was suddenly Sunday in his mind.

-- Chris Stiebens

Inner Landscapes

I am a long beach with fog drifting
coldly down the flat sand, the sun
can't break through to warm the air,
tiny sanderlings run up and down
following the quiet lapping
of this calm sea.

I pull my sweater closer
around my neck and keep walking
to the rhythm of the waves with tiny
drops of salt in my hair.

Make me this long foggy beach:
the air swirling damp and gray even at noon,
my footsteps disappearing in the wet surf,
pools left behind the mussel-crusted rocks
where my thoughts collect at low tide
like closed anemones, and gulls cry
their pains in the oppressed air
of salt drops and seaweed.

-- Emily Strauss

Crush of Waves

Like oceanic shipping containers
let loose in the sea, steel pounding
with their thousands of tons
the impact when they hit shakes
the ground, the force so deep the air
bows with sound all night
through my sleep.

So immense its cover of earth
The ocean warps from
gravitational
planetary
forces, then quiets suddenly as it
recedes, pulling itself back down
its sandy shelf, slinking away
to collect its strength before it rears
again, waiting to crush steel fists
against rock, to disturb my sleep.

-- Emily Strauss

Tropical tempest

Flash floods warnings in Kauai and Oahu—

In Honolulu, the rains got heavy,
pouring off corrugated steel roofs like waterfalls.

A maid dashed across my hotel's poolside
carrying fresh towels under her umbrella.

Along slippery rock-surfaced sidewalks,
pedestrians dodged puddles alongside curbs,
their sandaled feet soaked.

One night,
claps of thunder sounded like explosions,
lightning flashes turned skies bright.

Deserted beaches, restaurant patios closed ...

definitely not paradise.

-- Bonnie Quan Symons

Seaweed on the Beach

Reds, greens, browns, and mustard yellow
add earthy undertones,
the taste of miso,
to the neons, the overexposed
blues and whites and yellows,
the painted plaques and t-shirts,
the stick candies and salt-water taffy
sold at the gift store.

The rusty Irish moss
on this beach
will not turn into
anemones or coral
or even amber sea glass.
Like the seagull accents
wheeling in the wind
past summer,
the moss remains.

-- Marianne Szlyk

Find Your Beach Where It Is

I.

In Greenland,
children play past midnight
on a rocky beach
without sand or seaweed.
Nearby flowers and lichens appear,
brightly wearing down boulders.
Tourists' tents bubble on sand
like orange and green fungi
on a fallen log.

They do not squander summer.

II.

The children in New England
fling ribbons of brown seaweed
and streamers of green
back into the water.

Adults swaddled in
gift store cover-ups
avoid the Atlantic's bite
and the seaweed that clings
to every wader's legs.

III.

The young father and his sons
fish from the banks of the river
his grandfather once swam in.
It was clean. It was decent.
He recalls from his wheelchair.

Sun sparkling on the water,
the green flourishing on the bank,
the white of new polo shirts,
hide dangers in the fish
that swim this river
the color of a great-grandfather's memory.

-- Marianne Szlyk

Sand Man

Fred Connors was a man most everyone has seen. He spends most of his time on the beach with his metal detector, looking for lost treasure of the active proletariat. Over the years he has accumulated many valuable things...enough in fact to cover the cost of his solid state treasure retrieving device.

In addition to the exercise treasure hunting offered, his tan and his white hair gave him a sharp look that was so popular with the ladies. His friendly manner and gift-of-gab made him quite noticeable as he walked the sandy beach outside his well kept home. He had been a treasure hunter for about five years and liked the process the sand and the sun. Much of what he discovered was just cans and trash and he would wonder why he invested money in a machine that never seemed to uncover anything of real value. The real payoff was the healthy life-style and friends he made walking the beach. Today would be the day he found the best find ever, he kept saying to himself as he made his way to the white sand.

"Good morning Fred." said Elmer, a long time friend and neighbor as they passed.

"Oh yea...good morning." he replied as he almost missed the greeting. He was trying to remain concentrated on the area had mapped out to search. Feeling very good about his new search he turned on his machine and started walking. Clouds were gathering and providing some welcome shade and unfortunately a bit of rain, forcing him to seek shelter for a while. This would not discourage him though. This was his day and nothing would deter him from his goal. The rain was short lived and soon he was up and searching again.

The first few nibbles were beer cans as usual but nothing was going to discourage him today.

This new area, was two houses down from his own and after searching for about an hour, his machine started howling rather loudly. He had found the treasure he thought he would. Digging down just three or four inches revealed something shiny gold. he managed to get his hand on it and lifted it out of the hole. It was a gold cigarette case.

"Find something?" came a voice from behind.

"No...just another crushed beer can." he replied to the stranger.

"Well, good luck." said the man as he walked away.

This was special, so he decided to take it home and see what he had discovered. The walk seemed for ever but finally he stood in front of his door. The first piece of business was to relax and cool down with a cold beer. His heart was beating fast as he took deep breath and closed his eyes for a few seconds. What had he found, he wondered as he caught his breath and prepared to open his eyes and discover the treasure. It was a gold cigarette case and it looked quite expensive. There was something in in it he could see, paper it appeared. It was a letter and it was addressed to him. What could this possibly be? The letter read:

Dear Fred:

My name is Jenny and I'm 14 years old. I met you on the beach once and you looked like such a nice man I thought you would make a great father. My step-father isn't so great.

He is going to kill me. I managed to find my mothers cigarette case some paper and a pencil. Right now I am chained to the bed but I can manage to write this. I can't get away and he says he will kill me and bury me outside in the sand.

I have been swallowing jewelry and anything metal. I buried this for you to find when my step-father let me outside for a few minutes. Please look for me with your machine.

He was startled and shocked and ready to pick up his machine and go hunting for something he must find. Furiously he ran to the place where she said and ran the machine over the sand in desperation. An hour passed and then two and had to sit. He was exhausted but soon was back searching as he cried. How could this happen he kept asking himself? Then the machine started buzzing loudly and he fell to his knees and started digging with his hands. What ever it was, it was deep and then he felt something fleshy.

It was her. he grabbed what felt like an arm and pulled. It was indeed an arm of a young girl.

Crying as he pulled her from the ground, it had proved to be to much for his heart. He stood motionless for a moment, crying and shaking with grief and guilt for not being able to save this precious young girl.

Then he collapsed and someone passing by called the police. Soon there were police and ambulances all around. They managed to revive Fred and after a week or so in the hospital, he returned home.

Still, Fred liked the beach and the beautiful sunsets but his treasure hunting days were over, for he had found the treasure of his life...the daughter who had adopted him.

-- *Terence Thomas*

A Waltz on the Beach

Moonbeams lapped the lonely shoreline as raucous children, barking dogs and shouting adults fled the dark for pizza and the fun house. Thousands of tiny crabs waltzed for survival in the sand, each searching for that left over morsel of sustenance.

The surf crashed onto the sand carrying eerie white ghosts on top of each breaker. The ghosts evaporated into millions of bubbles and were drawn back into the infinite ocean.

And thus did the soul of Mary Potter come ashore that night. Her soul did not immediately dissolve into tiny bubbles. Rather, Mary Potter settled into a hole dug by a father and son and waited.

***

Colleen Murphy and her family lived year round at the shore. Her father owned a small but profitable fleet of fishing vessels. He sailed that night with a group of businessmen from New York City.

She peered towards the lights on the horizon and wondered which one belonged to her father. She could call him, of course, but he would never understand what brought her alone to the beach at midnight.

She waded ankle deep in the warm water lost in a despair that only a teenage girl can feel. The love of her life left her humiliated and afraid. She gave herself to Matt and then he walked, nay, ran away from her.

"What if I'm pregnant?" she cried alone on the beach.

Coleen could not yet know for sure but in their passion the condom remained in Matt's shorts. She looked to the depths for an answer. She took a step into the surf and then retreated to the safety of the beach. But the warmth and the quiet of the deep called her name. The black ocean promised her peace and she desperately wanted to accept the invitation.

As Colleen danced through the shallows, she stepped on the soul of Mary Potter. Colleen stumbled in the hole and Mary's bubble burst around Colleen's feet and legs as a mist floated to her nose and mouth. The teenager tasted the whirling mist on her tongue and it crept into her nostrils as she absorbed the soul of the dead woman.

Mary felt warmth for the first time in two centuries. She gazed up and down the beach trying to understand what brought her here. She looked at clothes that were not hers and at young hands and feet. She breathed deeply and stretched and gave a howl of sheer joy to be alive again.

The old woman who died in a shipwreck lived now, a teenager again with a new world in front of her.

Colleen's head ached in confusion. When she took a step she fell to the sand. She tried to say a word but a howl erupted from her lips. Her eyes saw hands and feet that were old and shriveled.

Colleen decided that she fell asleep on the sand. She vaguely remembered a dream about an old woman and an ancient sailing vessel. In her dream a violent storm appeared out of nowhere and ripped the sails to shreds. The terror of falling into the ocean and of drowning seemed absolutely real.

Mary Potter was puzzled. She knew she was telling her story but to whom. Slowly the consciousness of Mary Potter and Colleen Murphy merged into a single body, each being vaguely aware of the other. And soon Mary Potter and Colleen Murphy became almost indistinguishable.

As predator and prey battled for survival in the seas, the souls of the women battled for the body of Colleen in an endless dance of embrace and rejection that flowed into day and then into weeks.

Then Colleen's body betrayed her.

The shame crushed the teenager but Mary rejoiced. She bore a new life. Colleen's body, young and strong, could birth the child. Mary's love, experience, wisdom, and new strength would provide for a child.

The dance of the souls stopped. The musicians took a break. Their instruments fell silent. Couples left the dance floor. Only Mary and Colleen remained. Silently they glided into a graceful waltz.

And arm in arm they reached an agreement.

They went back to their beach on a warm summer night. Colleen relaxed. Her soul loosened its grip. Mary reached out gently and Colleen cried a tear. A breeze came up and blew Colleen's mist into the waiting sea and to eternity.

-- Tim Tobin

Yankee Iron-ee. cummings

I have trouble with the concept of elite schools
Incredibly grandiose
Snobbish hotels
As I vacation here in this exclusive resort
Where I question my sanity —
(Park the car please thank you)

And as I sit here observing the mundane expressions
Frowned wrinkles amidst the gaiety of waxed bosoms
Spitting and seasoning themselves on skewers of opulence
Rotating on diamonds without respite
Roasted
Yet bereft of any warmth —
(Yes please have the boat bring us back by 3 thank you)

I question
(While eating my posh fish sandwich)
How anyone could be a grouch in this dazzling world
Of red onions
Mushroom-sprouting pools
Pickles on the side
(Yes another please waiter thank you)
Wondering how they can be so piggish
(Charge it to the room please thank you)

-- Christine Tsen

Jawing

Yes sweetie, five sharks
At the beach we're heading to in Chatham –
        I like 'em!
Great Whites, huge thirty foot charmers
Ghostly shadows of the sea –
        If a shark attacks me, I'll just punch 'im in
        the nose!
That's why the harbor master closed South Beach
Sharks are voracious death dealers, see
Masterful at cutting ---
        I'll pull on his teeth, pull 'em right out--
        And they'll just pop-pop
        Then, I'll—
        Punch his nose and what kind of sharks are
        they again?
Their teeth are shaped by nature
Engineered by the Divine
And they have an insatiable appetite
        I'm hungry Mom--
They were coming in for the seals, rapid fire
One nearly swallowed a little girl yesterday
White Death --
But they also give life
By making sure only the strong survive—
        I'll just punch 'im in the nose
        Give 'im a bloody nose
        So his shark friends'll come and eat 'im
        They'll think he's prey
        Then they'll give each OTHER bloody noses
        And they'll all eat each other's noses
        And they'll all go extinct--
It's the circle of life, drenched and orbiting
See, sharks compete with man for domination
Of the sea, the beaches
And (are you still buckled?) they instill fear
Like humans they have no predator ----

> *Wait-- if sharks eat seals, and seals eat fish, does*
> *Man eat sharks?*

And so their relationship with man
Is a curious one of hunter and hunted,
> *Does a woman eat 'em too?*

One alternating with the other.
> *I like 'em!*

           -- Christine Tsen

Kovalenko's Zen

We met each sunset
on the sand at Santa Cruz
that summer,
you with your staff –
stick, pipe, flute and knife –
and your rumbling laughter.

In the hills behind Soquel
you took me to the bees,
sitting zazen session
near the hives,
quiet lessons;

how time flies.

I looked for you
after the earthquake –
you'd gone somewhere
I couldn't reach.

I carry a stick
when I walk the beach, now,
as we turn towards the dark.

No blade, no flute, no pipe –
just a stick
to write sand haiku,
snacks for greedy waves.

You taught me
to centre twice a day.
I gave your gifts away so I could keep them.

Did another earthquake take you
or a trip to Mexico on someone else's yacht?
I imagine you throwing dice with Rumi,

Rilke and Rimbaud, everyone laughing
at a joke about the medium
and the massage. I don't get it.

I talk to you at sunset on the beach.
Sunrise is for someone else.

-- Mercedes Webb-Pullman

Self-Serve

totara stick
poked between rocks
low tide on a West Coast beach

sea surge
about my thighs

sudden weight
of catch

slow

careful
withdrawal

triumph; angry clack
of slick black skitter
in the tin

boiled in seawater
red legs cracked
sweet salty flesh extracted

feast

-- Mercedes Webb-Pullman

Scenes from California

I. Elk In Fog

To think that diaphanous fog
could obscure
so massive a creature
silhouetted against the horizon
as if far away,
while the ocean, veiled in mists,
roared against the cliffs.

II. Trapped Cow

Somehow it slipped
down the muddy gully
and couldn't climb out.
A man out hiking
heard the bellowing
and summoned the farmer
who shot the animal
out of mercy.
Surprisingly preserved,
its body leans
against the incline
like a black shadow,
its unseen feet resting
in shallow water.

III. Life/Land Forms

The slopes of the headlands
slide smoothly to the sea
of cold waters and roiling tides.

Under a wet shock of brown grass,
the narrow skeleton of a fox,
where weeds blow back yellow and russet,

and coots align in even rows
across the rippling surface of a pond.

Past mossy trees tangled in vines
and lichen-covered fences of an old farm,
lies a ribbon of brown sand
without beginning or end.

-- Anne Whitehouse

A Girl Who Fell in Love with an Island

I thought I saw the ghost of myself
as I was at the age of 27,
standing up on a bicycle, peddling uphill,
long hair streaming behind her.
She smiled as she passed me in the twilight
and wished me a good evening.

On the back of her bike was
a milk crate for hauling things,
the same as I once had.
She was wearing flip-flops
and a loose wrapped skirt.
I had seen her on the beach,
making salutations to the setting sun
over the sea in a reflected fire
of blazing gold and rose embers.
I hadn't wanted to interrupt her,
or show her to herself thirty years older.

I was a girl who fell in love with an island.
Each time I've left here,
something of that quiet, introspective girl
has lingered behind and never left.
On visits when I come across her
she has never gotten any older.

In August I return in search of her,
wearing my oldest clothes, ones she wore,
worn and faded, softened by use.
Once again she and I are one
when I swim in the cove's cold waters,
gazing up at the sea and sky
or diving underwater to watch
the dark kelp waving over the rocks.

-- Anne Whitehouse

Songs for the End of August

I

The weather suddenly turns,
a new wind blows in,
and summer, which had
scarcely seemed endurable,
becomes its most beguiling,
the breeze cool and fresh,
as if it were spring again.
Dew glistens in the grass,
and bird and insect songs fill the air.

Come out in the morning with me,
while the morning is still young,
let's walk and run and swim and bike,
use all our muscles, and then sit still,
taking everything in.

II

I'm bleaching my clothes in the sun.
the stains of the past year
that I could scarcely see
in indoor illumination
are fading in the strong sunlight,
fierce yet forgiving, where
even I will soak myself a while.

III

Taking the long view,
I regard the lighthouse
across the wide, wide Sound,
where sailboats rest at anchor on this sparkling day.
A long line of puffed-up clouds
promenades regally over the horizon,

and the sea ripples over and over itself,
whispering, *Not yet, not yet.*

        IV

Chased by sparrows,
a hawk flies low into the bushes.
A breeze rustles in the aspen leaves,
ruffling green over white, white over green.
From an oak branch
hangs a rope swing,
its end twisted in a knot,
waiting for a rider.

        -- Anne Whitehouse

Nostalgia

I am what is missing
from yesterday's photograph.
You can clearly make out
blue swimming trunks
concealing what once were legs.
You can tell there should be arms
to keep her from falling.

Behind: an ocean
folding and breaking.
The sun: leaving its mark
on the absence of a body.
Everywhere: a pit, so like love,
rimmed in faltering light.

This is what remains
of that summer by the sea:
her figure forever leaning into open air
and the sand wearing my ghost
like a broken window.

-- John Sibley Williams

Holiday

It's our bones that dry and crumble
and peek through our children's curious toes

mid-summer with the sun turning marrow to sand
to the glass of a fractured mirror

an expanse of family stretched raw over miles
diluted by grains of ancestors and distance

molded together for an hour into castles
then flatted by our sons just before the sea arrives

-- John Sibley Williams

Tarot: Moon with Water and Crab

Here is the hidden psychic power, emerging from water.
You are about to embark on a purposeful journey.
This pilgrimage to the divine, is unclear,
for it is coming out of an exoskeleton of darkness.
Your subconscious knows what you are searching for,
but it is hidden from you. Leave when the moon is full,
and scuttle across dreams, tender as a lover
carrying their soul. Water is slippery for interpretation.

Ask yourself: what is distracting you?
The moon can drown in water, but a crab can climb out.
Can you silence the thoughts barking out commands?

We have two kinds of rivers. One is cleansing,
and the other is muddy. Which you travel will depend
if you can use a half-moon as a boat,
or if you grasp at nothing with crab-like hands.

Ask yourself: what is drifting away?

-- Martin Willitts, Jr.

On Entering

I.

Entering has always remained
The easier of the two.

When sea crescent odes are sang
To chimera moons; forged
with a symmetry only the most
opaque and puerile seas
could reflect.

Door
      Lace
            Novel
                  Mouth

Inside
      In-between

Zoo
      Museum
            Drunkenness
                   Labyrinth

Virgin
      Harlot
            Carriage
                   Immortality

II.

The rotunda in Spain,
Where the panacea and soporific
Caused so much awe and panic.
     (remember the minotaur in the sand?)

The cathedral temples
Where ideas of martyrdom
First blossomed.

The cinema house,
Where you caught yourself
between the word and the light.

(*Apollonian acts and a Baroque Dionysus*)

An olive grove
        Next to water
Where you were born and learned
        To sing "Laila Laila."

The billet near the Dead Sea,
Where you could no longer distinguish
Between "garden," "library,"
"siesta," "blood."

And along the castle valley next to your bed,
    Where junipers and peonies raise their walls
To obstruct all ghosts and madmen
    From the dream-sand of martyrs.

              -- *Matthew Wylie*

A Few Words Near the Boardwalk and a Star

I.

       Follow the steps and arrows forward –
I think it will take you to where Alejandra wants to find the sharks.
    (*and this will serve like a lantern to your kisses*):

II.

Adora wants to die in the United States,
    But Gulf of Mexican rock and sentiment won't let her.

Marcus wants to become an incunabulist,
    So that pyramids look like seashells or things he finds in the half-light.

We still haven't figured out what Reyes wants because his fingers (*lemon snarls*)
    are always too close to the strings of the solitary mandolin
    kept by his bedside near the sea.

And if Helen arrives, she will most likely bring the only novella
    she is reading and impressively burning,
    (*along with her wardrobe*)

As for Graciana, we didn't find what we were looking for,
    only nine torn papers outlining the archetype of her Father.

    "5 degrees to the left and then cut a 180 degree angle.
    Afterwards, wash your hands of it in the salt-red water and sleep."

III.

I was taught through proverb and poem that this would take me
    to where Alejandra found the sharks,

hoping that the bits of rooftops we walked upon
would occasionally fall like rain and hell in my heart.

-- Matthew Wylie

A Few Questions for the Ocean

    Why can tonight *not*
Have stars that accompany each other
And remain dressed in basil laden furs
That catch water from rain
And golden moonlight
    And *Romeo and Juliet*
And mesquite firewood

    Crackling
Next to your ear

So that everything on water could be music
Or the birth of painting
    Or the fires of canvas
Sharks have stored in their
    Lantern eyes?

                  -- Matthew Wylie

Reflection: After the Great Wave

Come
forget
how loss feels
like a vast door closed
on the promise of dry land
or a window overlooking tsunami
damage so severe even our precious language fails

until revenge filigrees your hair like light, like nails
tearing at your eyes and flesh as you tell me
you wish you could understand
why pale bodies rose:
children, seals,
egrets,
foam.

-- Robert Wynne

Bolsa Chica State Beach

Driving south on PCH, windows down
and the Pacific Ocean exhales
its salty breath. I remember being thrown

into that water, high school weekends
crowded around a fire pit
waiting to see how long a soda could last

before the flames coaxed it into a geyser.
Coat hangers gave their lives
for hot dogs and marshmallows

only to end up bent, charred
and hoarding heat in cool gray ash.
The aroma is acrid and nostalgic

as it reaches the street, and I remember
sand between my toes, waves tickling foam
across my feet, moonlight bathing

my pale form. The scent intoxicates
but I always forget how lonely I was
on that beach, how certain

I would never be happy enough
to remember Coke splashing down,
pooling in the flickering glow

while all the couples snuck away
to dark lifeguard towers
and I drew words in wet sand,

watched the tide carry them away
like a promise.

-- Robert Wynne

One Red Umbrella

A hairy insect lands on my bare foot
as the lifeguard descends from Tower #1
to stand in the sunny spot between

a palm tree's shadow and the surf.
No one is occupying volleyball court #3
but several people have crowded around

one red umbrella near the shore,
where the coarse sand encases
their buried toes like a loving reminder

of how fickle whispering water is
compared to such generous clouds.

-- Robert Wynne

Amelia Island

An old man with a pot belly sagging over his black trunks,
Twirls an opened striped umbrella as he wades into the sea.
Not more than a mile away, a storm approaches,
Turning both the sea and sky the color of an old bruise.

Though the warm, rough waves smash against his hairless chest,
He holds the umbrella above his head, high and dry.
Then he turns, laughing, and slowly wades back to shore.
On the sand, he closes the umbrella and bows to the sea,

And accepts the crashing of the surf as applause.

-- Ron Yazinski

Off Key West, Hemingway Sails with Homer

This evening,
Even my life insurance doesn't reassure me of my worth.
I am left conceiving my death for my sixty-first year.
Then others will imagine how I rode the high tide of this wine-dark sea,
Singing myself now like one of the men fated to be devoured by Scylla,
An expendable sailor who had peeked ahead in the poem and so knew his fate.

I confess to the sea the gulls and the sun,
How tired I am of all this dreaming,
Of plunging a knife in our captain's back and throwing his body overboard
Just to say I could.
But I know I'll never awaken from this poem.

And every rosy-fingered dawn,
The master still walks the deck, shouting orders, encouraging our hearts.
My only comfort is my knowledge of Scylla,
Which no one believes,
Especially my comrades who are destined to join me.
They ask me why I seem so sober,
Now that the swells are taking us home;
They laugh and tease me that I just miss the killing.
That's right, I tell them.
A good cry would make me feel better,
Especially if it's not my own.

-- Ron Yazinski

Freshfield Beach

Even now, the childhood pleasure:
warm sand thrusting between the toes,
trousers rolled to the knee
and the gentle swirl of wavelets
undermining my feet.

The tide is drawing back, leaving
sky splashed behind the sand-bars
and augers lying empty, as if unicorns,
plunging among the breakers' foam,
had lost their horns, and drowned.

-- Mantz Yorke

From The Editors

Heliophile

Rays, full of nourishing
melatonin, massage muscles,
pigment pallid skin. Sand's sacrifice,
I am lying, prone offering to God
of the golden eye. Willing
embodiment of indolence, I emulate
coma as I breathe in the warming
embrace of cosmic fire, become phoenix
emerging from strangling hold
of winter's ashen cocoon.

-- A.J. Huffman

Red Tide

Light bleeds across salted waters, fills
the air with fatality. Eyes cannot adjust
to the tragic beauty of beached bodies,
mouthing voiceless words. There is a unity
to this funereal display, various corpses
flailing in synchronized portrait of death.
The frame frills with universal callousness.
God's lack of discrimination reflects harshly
against quiet whispers of receding waves.

-- A.J. Huffman

The Fishermen

Reclined visions of hat-covered faces and
bare feet digging into sand, these elderly men
have perfected the art of breathing in still-life
portrait. Minutes drag into hours. Sometimes
wind will dislodge a brim, force a hand to readjust.
Most passersby think they are sleeping, maybe even dead,
until familiar *whizzzz* of line running activates them.
They sprint from chairs like twenty-somethings,
actual age regressing in excitement of ensuing battle.
Previously hidden biceps now bulge
through t-shirts quickly darkening with sweat.
They tug, jerk, pull, anything to set hook into nibbling
mouth. Instinct tells them it has. They relax, returning
heart rates to normal as they reel in the morning's catch.

-- A.J. Huffman

There is Something Wrong

with the image of a frozen beach, fresh
powdered snow, a bleaching blanket of white
smothering the soft peach-toned grains. I remember
walking to the water's edge, disturbed
by how different my prints looked in January.
Heavy, rounded by treds, indistinguishable from
those of other onlookers. In June they would be alive,
each five-toed print a perfect portrait of a foot
that could only be mine. I sighed as I looked out
onto the frigid chunked mass of Lake Erie.
My eyes attempted to blink away a snapshot
of what others heralded as light-frosted beauty, but I
only saw the stagnant suffocation of warm
memories, the squalid bluster silencing childhood
laughter.

-- A.J. Huffman

Squirrels on the Beach

There are no nuts here
to be foraged, at least
not the edible ones. Just a few
unfortunate almost-escapees
peeking from too-small Speedos.
And yet twin tails twitch
at the edge of the tide. Perhaps
testing their timing. They leap
frog sand, shells, each
other to maintain their distance
from the onslaught
of/and the waves.

-- A.J. Huffman

A Woman on the Beach that is Now a Stranger

It has been twenty years and I can no longer
conjure her salty taste, the way she wet the skin
of soft sand with gentle, rhythmic tongues,
opened herself to the sun in silent worship,
the overwhelming noise she made when she came
inland, over and over. She let me lie
against her vast expanse for so long my body
made an imprint into hers, then she washed it away,
a delicate removal of our evidence. My hair
tangled with the seaweed of hers until I thought
we may never resume our own boundaries.

-- April Salzano

Dragging the Ocean

onto the beach, the moon recedes
behind cover of cloud. All castles
erased, a desolate shore waits
for shells to be washed and picked
by selective hands. I find the one
conch without voice, a speechless mouth
below unicorn horn. Vacated.
There is no noise pink enough
to void silence this loud.

-- April Salzano

Bathtub Conclusions

You have grown. Stretched
out, you are the length of the tub
that once seemed an ocean
with carpet shore, lightbulb sun.
This windless beach has lost
its wonder, grown smaller. Shallow
water holds no treasure
of discovered toes, every day new
again. The triumph of staying
upright, lost like a sailboat
shampoo bottle, magic of mirror.

-- April Salzano

My Kids Think Lake Erie is the Ocean

Sad commentary on our northerness.
We are not water people. We don't go
boating or skimming the surface on skis.
I do not enjoy the suffocating
feel of water over my head, tunneled
sound, slow motion movement, my own
buoyancy. The ocean scares me, hot
sand, pinching stinging creatures, undrinkable
water everywhere, pale skin turning
into tight red exterior, freckling with melanoma.
Waves, they say, and, *look how big
the ocean is*. They ask if there are sharks here.
Yes, I say, and, be careful. Stay close.
Guilt crashes over me, drags me under
where I neither sink nor swim.

-- April Salzano

Remains

Water folded in on sand, washing
away thousands of granules as it receded.
Each time, less beach.
Each time, the wetness coming closer
to touching my skin. A hard wind forced
shells deeper into hiding. Somewhere
on Lake Erie, waves rolled higher, pulled
by a full moon with nothing to blink at.
Moaning gulls cried in human voices.
It was not my virginity that was taken
with foaming crest, thrown to open beaks,
but it may as well have been.

-- April Salzano

Author Bios

Pamela Ahlen is program director for Bookstock (Woodstock, Vermont), a Festival of Words, one of three Vermont literary festivals. She has organized literary readings for ILEAD (Institute for Lifelong Education at Dartmouth). Pam received an MFA in creative writing from Vermont College of Fine Arts. Her poems have most recently appeared in *Bloodroot*, *Birchsong* and *The Sow's Ear*. She is the author of the chapbook *Gather Every Little Thing*.

Barbara Bald is a retired teacher, educational consultant and freelance writer. Her poems have been published in a variety of anthologies: *The Other Side of Sorrow, The 2008* and *2010 Poets' Guide to New Hampshire* and *For Loving Precious Beast*. They have appeared in *The Northern New England Review, Avocet, Off the Coast* and in multiple issues of The Poetry Society of New Hampshire's publication: *The Poets' Touchstone*. Her work has been recognized in both national and local contests including the Rochester Poet Laureate Contest, Lisbon's Fall Festival of Art Contest, Conway Library's Annual Contest, Goodwin Library's Annual Contest, and The Poetry Society of New Hampshire's National and Member Contests. Her recent full-length book is called *Drive-Through Window* and her new chapbook is entitled *Running on Empty*. Barb lives in Alton, NH with her cat Catcher, two Siamese Fighting fish and a tank of Hissing Cockroaches.

Linda Bearss has published a variety of poems as well as articles on Theodore Roethke and Paul Laurence Dunbar. Ms. Bearss is a poet/writer, who teaches literature and composition for high school and college students. She has earned master degrees in English language and literature from Central Michigan University and the University of Michigan-Flint. Ms. Bearss is also a member of the National Writing Project, Society for the Study of Midwestern Literature, and Academy of American Poets.

James Bell has published two poetry collections. The second, *fishing for beginners (2010)* like the first *the just vanished place (2008)* was published by *tall-lighthouse*. He currently lives in France where he contributes articles to an English language journal and continues to write and publish poetry worldwide.

Most recently he has been a guest editor for *Transparent Words* the online poetry magazine that is part of Poetry Kit.

Byron Beynon lives in Swansea, Wales. His work has appeared in several publications including Jellyfish Whispers, Chicago Poetry Review, Camel Saloon, London Magazine, The Worcester Review, The Independent and The Interpreter's House. He has been coeditor of the poetry magazine Roundyhouse. He was also involved in coordinating Wales' contribution to the poetry anthology Fifty Strong (Heinemann). A Pushcart Prize nominee. A new book of poems, The Echoing Coastline, is forthcoming from Agenda Editions (UK).

Doug Bolling whose poetry is both experimental and somewhat traditional, has appeared in numerous literary reviews including Trajectory, Poetalk, Hurricane Review, Water-Stone Review, Blue Unicorn, Indefinite Space, Tribeca Poetry Review and Basalt among others. He has received three Pushcart Prize nominations and currently resides outside Chicago in Flossmoor, Illinois.

Nancy Brashear loves poetry and has been reading and writing it from a young age. Born in a Southern California beach city, she loves nothing more that hearing the sound of surf. Recent publications include an original re-told fairytale, academic articles on literature and literacy development, and web-work for publishers, and she has also participated in poetry and short story readings.

Bob Brill is a retired computer programmer and digital artist. He is now devoting his energies to writing fiction and poetry. His novellas, short stories and more than 100 poems have appeared in more than two dozen online magazines, print journals, and anthologies.

Michael H. Brownstein has been widely published. His latest works include Firestorm: A Rendering of Torah (http://booksonblog35.blogspot.com/) (Camel Saloon Books on Blogs) and The Katy Trail, Mid-Missori, 100F Outside and other poems (http://barometricpressures.blogspot.com/2013/07/the-katy-trail-mid-missouri-100f.html) (Barometric Pressures--A Kind of Hurricane Press). His work has appeared in The Café

Review, American Letters and Commentary, Xavier Review, Hotel Amerika, Meridian Anthology of Contemporary Poetry, The Pacific Review, and others. In addition, he has nine poetry chapbooks including The Shooting Gallery (Samidat Press, 1987), Poems from the Body Bag (Ommation Press, 1988), A Period of Trees (Snark Press, 2004), What Stone Is (Fractal Edge Press, 2005), and I Was a Teacher Once (Ten Page Press, 2011: (http://tenpagespress.wordpress.com/2011/03/27/i-was-a-teacher-once-by-michael-h-brownstein/). He is the editor of First Poems from Viet Nam (2011).

Lesley Burt lives in Christchurch, Dorset, UK. She retired from social work education in 2009 and has been writing poetry for about 12 years. Her poems have been published online, in magazines and anthologies, including: Tears in the Fence, Poetry Nottingham, The Interpreter's House, Roundyhouse, Dorset Voices, and in the recent Robin Hood Book, edited by Alan Morrison. She has received awards in competitions, including the Bedford Open 2011, the Alan Sillitoe Open 2012, Christchurch Writers' Poetry Competition 2009 & 2010, and the Virginia Warbey 2012. She also wrote a chapter for: Teaching Creative Writing, edited by Elaine Walker (2012), Professional and Higher Partnership. Since retirement she has run a poetry group on a voluntary basis, with the aim of promoting the enjoyment of reading and writing poetry in her local community.

Fern G.Z. Carr is a lawyer, teacher and past president of the local branch of the BC Society for the Prevention of Cruelty to Animals. She is a member of The League of Canadian Poets and former Poet-in-Residence who composes and translates poetry in five languages. A winner of national and international poetry contests, Carr has been published extensively world-wide from Finland to Mayotte Island in the Mozambique Channel. Canadian honours include being featured online in Canada's national newspaper, The Globe and Mail, having her poetry set to music by a Juno-nominated musician and having her poem, "I Am", chosen by the Parliamentary Poet Laureate as *Poem of the Month* for Canada. www.ferngzcarr.com

Beth Copeland had her second book *Transcendental Telemarketer* (BlazeVOX books, 2012) receive the runner up award in the North Carolina Poetry Council's 2013 Oscar Arnold Young Award for best poetry book by a North Carolina writer. Her first book *Traveling through Glass* received the 1999 Bright Hill Press Poetry book Award. Two of her poems have been nominated for a Pushcart Prize. Copeland is an English instructor at Methodist University in Fayetteville. She lives with her husband Phil Rech in a log cabin in Gibson, North Carolina.

Linda M. Crate is a Pennsylvanian native born in Pittsburgh, but she was raised in the rural town of Conneautville. She attended and graduated from Edinboro University of Pennsylvania with a degree in English-Literature in 2009. Her poetry, articles, reviews, and short stories have appeared in several journals online and in print. Her poetry chapbook *A Mermaid Crashing Into Dawn* was recently published by Fowlpox Press.

Chris Crittenden blogs as Owl Who Laughs. His full-length collection Jugularity was recently released by Stonesthrow Press.

Betsey Cullen resides in West Chester, Pennsylvania, having lived on the East Coast for most of her life. She earned her B.A. in history and her M.A. in education from the University of Rochester and Cornell University, respectively, and began studying and writing poetry after retiring from her professional fundraising career at Phillips Academy in Andover, Massachusetts. She is married and has two grown children and three granddaughters.

Oliver Cutshaw has published poetry, articles, and non-fiction works. He is currently writing a memoir of his father's career as a jockey in the heyday of the horse racing industry. Originally from the East Coast, his works frequently appeared in the literary journals and pop culture weeklies of the Boston area. He now resides in Southern California working as a librarian.

Susan Dale has had her poems and fiction published on *Eastown Fiction, Ken*Again, Hackwriters, Yesteryear Fiction, Feathered*

Flounder, and *Penwood Review*. In 2007, she won the grand prize for poetry from Oneswan.

Jessica de Koninck is a long-time resident of Montclair, New Jersey. The author of one collection, *Repairs,* her poems also appear in a variety of journals and anthologies including *The Ledge, The Valparaiso Poetry Review, the Paterson Literary Review* and elsewhere. She holds a B.A. from Brandeis and an M.F.A. from Stonecoast, U.S.M.

Hannah Dellabella currently studies at Carnegie Mellon University, where she double majors in Creative Writing and Professional Writing. She is a native of Bayonne, New Jersey, and is very aware of her Jersey accent. She is a compulsive imaginer.

Darren C. Demaree is living and writing in Columbus, Ohio with his wife and children. He is the author of "As We Refer to Our Bodies" (2013) and "Not For Art Nor Prayer" (2014), both are forthcoming from 8th House Publishing House. He is the recipient of two Pushcart Prize nominations.

Laura Dennis lives in Edmonton Alberta Canada. She has been published in two other anthologies, Home and Away by House of Blue Skies and Love Notes by Vagabond Press. She has two self-published chap books, Wheels on the Bus and The Bookshelf.

Andrea Janelle Dickens is from the Blue Ridge Mountains of Virginia and currently splits her time between Oxfordshire, England and Tempe, Arizona, where she teaches at Arizona State University. Her poems have appeared in New South Journal, The Found Poetry Review, Thin Air, and the Cobalt Review. She is also a beekeeper, gardener and ceramic artist in her spare time.

Richard Dyer has a number of short stories appearing in Pill Hill Press, Crow's Nest Magazine and Horror House. He also has a story appearing in an upcoming anthology, Whortleberry Press's *Dandelions on Mars*, a Ray Bradbury tribute. He resides at the Jersey shore with his wife, Susanne, and his son, Ian. He is a member of the Fictioneers, a science fiction writers group. He has also finished his book, *Drinkin' from the Hose*, a humorous collection of childhood adventures during the politically incorrect 1970's, which is currently being edited for publication.

Jim Eigo has written on theater, dance, art, literature, sex and the design of clinical trials. He helped design two reforms of AIDS drug regulation, accelerated approval and expanded access, that have helped bring many treatments to many people, work profiled in the recent Oscar-nominated documentary, *How to Survive a Plague*. His first published art work appears in a limited edition book from Intima Press, *The Poetics of Space*. His short fiction has appeared in such volumes as *Best American Gay Fiction #3*, in such periodicals as *The Chicago Review* and recently online at cleavermagazine.com. He blogs on Huffington Post.

Will Falk is a former Wisconsin Assistant State Public Defender living on the shore of Lake Michigan in the Bayview neighborhood of Milwaukee. Poetry helps him think. He can usually be found napping on a red granite stone that serves as the perfect couch in the South Shore Park off Trowbridge Street. If he has had too much coffee, he tries to talk to the orioles nesting above the lake. He would like to thank his mother, father, sister, and Tori for all of their support.

Kate Falvey lives by the sea in Long Beach with her fifteen year old daughter and teaches at City Tech in Brooklyn. Her poetry and fiction appear in a wide variety of print and online journals including Memoir(and), *Yellow Medicine Review*, *Revival* (Limerick Arts Center), *Danse Macabre, Subliminal Interiors, Hospital Drive, Citron Review* and many more. Her chapbooks, *What the Sea Washes Up* (Dancing Girl Press) and *Morning Constitutional with Sunhat and Bolero* (Green Fuse Press) are forthcoming soon. She is the editor in chief of the *2 Bridges Review* and on the editorial board of the *Bellevue Literary Review*.

Alexis Rhone Fancher is a member of Jack Grapes' L.A. Poets & Writers Collective. Her work has been published or is forthcoming in

RATTLE, BoySlut, The Mas Tequila Review, The Poetry Super Highway The Juice Bar, Cultural Weekly, High Coupe, Gutter Eloquence Magazine, Tell Your True Tale, Bare Hands, Downer Magazine, the anthology Poised In Flight and elsewhere. Her photographs have been published world-wide. In 2013 she was nominated for a Pushcart Prize. She is poetry editor of Cultural Weekly. http://www.alexisrhonefancher.com/

Elysabeth Faslund lives in Theriot, La., is an international, professional poet, changing with the times, but not the place. She believes the things she did in childhood and beyond, have become the stuff of her poetry She became the Louisiana Writers Society's Grand Prize winner of 1968. She is poet who has been internationally published since seventeen, and holds the Epic of Gesar a major work of literature, out-distancing the Bible by centuries.

Richard Fein was a finalist in The 2004 New York Center for Book Arts Chapbook Competition. A Chapbook of his poems was published by Parallel Press, University of Wisconsin, Madison. He has been published in many web and print journals such as: *Reed, Southern Review, Roanoke Review, Skyline Magazine, Birmingham Poetry Review, Mississippi Review, Paris/Atlantic, Canadian Dimension* and many others.

Joan Fishbein has had her work appear in *The New Verse News, The Origami Poems Project of Rhode Island, The Southern Poetry Anthology: Volume One, The Kennesaw Review, Poetry Super Highway, The Devil's Millhopper, Helicon Nine, The Reach of Song, The Frequency Anthology* and other small literary magazines. She lives in Providence, RI with her husband.

Neil Flatman is first an underwriter in the Lloyds of London insurance market but foremost a writer of prose and poems which occasionally don't make him want to hide all the knives in the house. He lives in Farnham in Surrey UK and has two teenage daughters. More of his poems can be found at: http://introvert-albino-unicyclist.blogspot.it/

Trina Gaynon has had her poems appear in the anthologies *Bombshells* and *Knocking at the Door*, as well as numerous journals including *Natural Bridge, Reed* and the final issue of *Runes*. Her chapbook *An Alphabet of Romance* is available from Finishing Line Press. Forthcoming publications in anthologies include: *A Ritual to Read Together: Poems in Conversation with William Stafford, Saint Peter's B-list: Contemporary Poems Inspired by the Saints, Obsession: Sestinas for the 21st Century*, and *Phoenix Rising from the Ashes: Anthology of Sonnets of the Early Third Millennium.*

Katie Hopkins Gebler teaches English at Diablo Valley College, Pleasant Hill, California, and has published in *The Writer Magazine, Anderbo*, and *The Blue Hour Anthology, Volume 2*.

Sue Mayfield Geiger is a freelance writer living on the Texas Gulf Coast. To view her publication credits, please visit her website: www.smgwriter.com.

Patricia L. Goodman is a widowed mother and grandmother and a Phi Beta Kappa graduate of Wells College with a B. A. in Biology. Her life has consisted of running an internationally known horse business with her orthodontist husband on their farm in Chadds Ford, PA; serving in many capacities in The American Trakehner Association; accompanying her husband on hunting trips around the world and very successfully raising four children. She now lives on the banks of the Red Clay Creek in Wilmington, close to the natural world she loves. She is a regular at Wilmington's Second Saturday Poets and has twice been a featured reader there. She is a member of Rehoboth Beach Writers Guild, Delaware Literary Connection, the Poetry Writing Workshop at the University of Delaware's Osher Lifelong Learning Institute and the Red Clay Poets workshop group. She has had poems published in *The Broadkill Review, Fox Chase Review, Aries, Requiem Magazine, Jellyfish Whispers, Sugar Mule, Your Daily Poem, The Weekly Avocet* and many anthologies and is completing her first full-length manuscript. Her poem *Snow at Midnight* won the 2013 Delaware Press Association Communications Award in the poetry division and placed second in the national NFPW contest. In the past five years Patricia has suffered three major losses, and claims her poetry has saved her sanity, helping her through these difficult times. Contact her at plgoodman@comcast.net.

Zélie Guérin is an avid reader, writer, and lover of poetry. She is also a psychic - tarot card reader and advisor.

Deborah Guzzi was born in Camden, Maine, U.S.A. She was educated at the University of Connecticut where she attained a Bachelor of Fine arts with equal focuses in Printmaking and Shakespeare. She first published at the age of sixteen. Ms. Guzzi has continued to work on her poetry throughout her sixty-four years. Using the inspiration gathered from her extensive travel. She has traveled in China, Nepal [during the civil war], Egypt [two weeks before The Arab Spring'] and most recently Peru. She has published works in the literary journals of Western Connecticut University. She has published two illustrated volumes of poetry, The Healing Heart and Heaven and Hell in a Nutshell. At the present, she writes articles for Massage and Aroma Therapy Magazines. Currently, she resides in Monroe, CT. She is owner operator of Empathic Touch. Acting as a healing facilitator, she specializes in the Eastern Arts of Shiatsu, Lomi Lomi, Thai Massage, Feng Shui and Reiki energetic healing.

Judy Hall is a teacher and writer in New Jersey. She is an MFA candidate at William Paterson University. She's been published in *Rose Red Review, Literary Orphans, Pyrokinection* and other national literary journals. She is currently writing a novel about a mother's struggle raising her bipolar son.

Dave Hardin is a Michigan poet and artist. His poems have appeared several times in *3 Quarks Daily* along with *The Prague Review*, *Drunken Boat, Hermes Poetry Journal, Epigraph Magazine, Loose Change, ARDOR, The Detroit Metro Times* and others. He contributes to Scrum, http://scrumsideup.blogspot.com, a blog of poetry and satire. Visual work is on display at http://jubileebarn.com/ In 2012 he self-published *A Ruinous Thirst,* a collection of poems. Contact him at

sgodnworb@yahoo.com or
https://www.facebook.com/ARuinousThirst.

William Ogden Haynes is a poet and author of short fiction from Alabama who was born in Michigan and grew up a military brat. His first book of poetry entitled *Points of Interest* appeared in 2012 and a second collection of poetry and short stories *Uncommon Pursuits* was published in 2013. Both are available on Amazon in Kindle and paperback. He has also published over sixty poems and short stories in literary journals and his work has been anthologized multiple times.

Damien Healy is from Dublin in Ireland but has lived in Osaka, Japan for the past twenty years. He holds an MA in Applied Linguistics and teaches English at university. He has co-written three textbooks for the Japanese market and has published several papers on teaching ESL. He has recently found the time to read and write poetry and short stories. He has been published in *The Weekenders, Spinozablue* and *The Ofipress* to name a few.

William D. Hicks lives in Chicago by himself (any offers?). Contrary to popular belief, he is not related to the famous comedian Bill Hicks (though he's just as funny in his own right). Hicks will someday publish his memoirs, but they will be about Bill Hicks' life. His poetry appears in *LITSNACK, Cannoli Pie, Outburst, The Legendary, Horizon* (Canada), *The Short Humour Site* (UK), *The Four Cornered Universe, Save the Last Stall for Me* and *Mosaic*.

Christopher Hivner lives in Pennsylvania , usually writes while listening to music and enjoys an occasional cigar outside on a star-filled night. He has recently been published in *Yellow Mama, Eye on Life Magazine, Dead Snakes* and *Illumen*. A book of horror short stories, *The Spaces between Your Screams* was published in 2008. You can connect with him on Twitter: @your_screams.

Liz Hufford dreams of "a kingdom by the sea" but lives in the desert. She writes articles, essays, poetry, and short stories. She has been published in *Dash, The Binnacle*, and *Poets Among Us/Aquillrelle 3*.

S.E. Ingraham writes from the 53rd parallel (Edmonton, AB, Canada) where she shares space with the love of her life plus an aging, chocolate-stealing border collie/wolf cross. In addition to writing, she levels pictures. Her work has appeared (or will soon) in: Shot Glass, The dVerse Anthology (Voices of Contemporary World Poetry), Poised in Flight, Red Fez, Pyrokinection, A Blackbird Sings, Storm Cycle - the Best of 2012 -- among others. More of her work may be found here: http://thepoet-tree-house.blogspot.ca/, here: http://seingrahamsays.wordpress.com/, and here: http://nsaynne.wordpress.com/

M. J. Iuppa lives on a small farm near the shores of Lake Ontario. Her most recent poems have appeared in *Poetry East*, *The Chariton Review*, *Tar River Poetry*, *Blueline*, *The Prose Poem Project*, and *The Centrifugal Eye*, among other publications. Her most recent poetry chapbook is *As the Crow Flies* (Foothills Publishing, 2008), and her second full-length collection is *Within Reach* (Cherry Grove Collections, 2010). *Between Worlds*, a prose chapbook, was published by Foothills Publishing in May 2013. She is Writer-in-Residence and Director of the Visual and Performing Arts Minor program at St. John Fisher College in Rochester, New York.

Miguel Jacq is a French-Australian poet/photographer/fiend. He lives with his wife in Melbourne, Australia, where he runs (some say ruins) an I.T business. His work has appeared in various online literary journals such as *Deep Water Journal*, *Jellyfish Whispers* and *Vox Poetica*, as well as in several printed anthologies by The Blue Hour Press and Dagda Publishing. In 2013 he published two poetry collections titled *Black Coat City* and *Magnetics*. He regularly writes at migueljacq.com.

Michael Lee Johnson lived ten years in Canada during the Vietnam era. Today he is a poet, freelance writer, photographer, and small business owner in Itasca, Illinois, who has been published in more than 750 small press magazines in twenty-five countries, he edits seven poetry sites. Poetry books: *The

Lost American: From Exile to Freedom (136 page book), several chapbooks, including *From Which Place the Morning Rises and Challenge of Night and Day, and Chicago Poems*. He has over 66 poetry videos on YouTube. Links to author website, book sales, and YouTube poetry videos: Authors website
http://poetryman.mysite.com/
http://www.lulu.com/spotlight/promomanusa
http://bookstore.iuniverse.com/Products/SKU-000058168/The-Lost-American.aspx http://www.amazon.com/The-Lost-American-Exile-Freedom/dp/0595460917
https://www.youtube.com/user/poetrymanusa/videos

Caroline Jones was born in Chester, UK, in 1981. Her poetry has been shortlisted for the Ravenglass Poetry Press competition 2012 (judged by Don Paterson) and published in the Ravenglass Poetry Press Anthology III. Her short-short fiction has appeared in *Flash: the International Short-short Story Magazine*, and she was awarded the Freeman and Guilds of the City of Chester Prize 2012 for her short story 'Sink or Swim'. She is currently writing a collection of fourteen-line poems.

Judith J. Katz is the Lead Teacher for Creative Writing at the Cooperative Arts and Humanities Magnet High School in New Haven, Connecticut, where her signature courses focus on writing poetry. Her work has been published in several print and online publications, including, The New Sound Literary Journal, Sending Our Condolences and The Yale New Haven Teacher's Institute. She is currently working on her first chapbook, entitled Blessings of Witnessing and Experience.

Claire Keyes is the author of two poetry collections: *The Question of Rapture* and the chapbook, *Rising and Falling*. Her poems and reviews have appeared most recently in *Literary Bohemia, Theodate, Crab Orchard Review,* and *Blackbird*. She lives in Marblehead, Massachusetts and is Professor Emerita at Salem State University.

Steve Klepetar teaches literature and creative writing at Saint Cloud State University in Minnesota. His latest book is *Speaking to the Field Mice*, published by Sweatshoppe Publications.

Craig Kyzar is an award-winning journalist and international attorney. After graduating from NYU Law School and enjoying eight years of legal practice in Manhattan, Craig is heavily involved in nonprofit work dedicated to enhancing children's literacy skills and connecting economically disadvantaged youth with a life-changing love of reading. His editorial columns and articles are regularly featured across several news outlets, providing uniquely provocative views on legal, political and humanitarian issues. His versatile poetry, personal essays and fictional work have been featured in national and international publications, including *Recovering the Self, The WiFiles, Green Heritage News, Houston News Online*, and the *Point Mass* anthology. Connect with Craig on Twitter at @ScriboLex.

Kate LaDew is a graduate from the University of North Carolina at Greensboro with a BA in Studio Art.

Duane Locke lives in Tampa, Florida near anhinga, gallinules, raccoons, alligators, etc. He has published 6,763 poems, includes 31 books of poems. His latest book publications: April 2012, DUANE LOCKE, THE FIRST DECADE, 1968-1978, BITTER OLEANDER PRESS. This book is a republication of his first eleven books, contains 333 pages. Order from http://www.bitteroleander.com/releases.html, Or Amazon. December 2012, his 31st was published TERRESTRIAL ILLUMINATIONS, FIRST SELECTION, 43 pages. by FOWLPOX PRESS, http://fowlpox.tk/

Michael Magee has had his poems and plays produced produced on BBC radio and on KSER FM (Pacifica Radio). His first book, "Cinders of my Better Angels" was published in 2011 by MoonPath Press. His poems and songs were produced by Mel/Munro on their CD "Vaudeville." He traces his roots to his grandfather in vaudeville and his mother who played honky-tonk stride piano. He waits by the beach sand running through his looking glass. While in England he worked for Billy Smart's Circus and his play "A Night in Reading Gaol with Oscar Wilde was produced in Derby. In America, his movie "Shank's Mare" won a best actor award at the Script to Screen Film Festival in Tulsa, Oklahoma.

Jacqueline Markowski has had her poetry appear in numerous publications including *Cochlea/The Neovictorian, Permafrost Literary Journal, The Camel Saloon, Pyrokinection* and *Jellyfish Whispers* and has been anthologized in "Backlit Barbell", "Storm Cycle" and "Point Mass" (Kind of a Hurricane Press*)*. Her short stories have appeared in *PoundofFlash.com*. She was awarded first place in poetry at The Sandhills Writers Conference. She is currently working on a compilation of short stories and a collection of poetry.

Carolyn Martin is happily retired in Clackamas, OR where she gardens, writes, and participates in communities of creative colleagues. Her first collection of poems, *Finding Compass*, was released in July, 2011. Currently, she is president of the board of directors of VoiceCatcher (www.voicecatcher.org), a nonprofit community that connects women writers and artists in greater Portland, OR/Vancouver, WA.

Austin McCarron has had his work recently appear in *Robin Hood Anthology, Ink, Sweat and Tears, Poetry Salzburg Review, Full of Crow* and others. He lives in London.

Joan McNerney has had her poetry included in numerous literary magazines such as *Seven Circle Press, Dinner with the Muse, Camel Saloon* Books on Blog, *Blueline, Barometic Pressure* E-book, *Spectrum,* three *Bright Spring Press Anthologies* and several *Kind of A Hurricane* Publications. She has been nominated three times for *Best of the Net*. Four of her books have been published by fine literary presses. She has recited her work at the National Arts Club, New York City, State University of New York, Oneonta, McNay Art Institute, San Antonio and other distinguished venues. A recent reading was sponsored by the American Academy of Poetry.

Her latest title is *Having Lunch with the Sky,* A.P.D. Press, Albany, New York.

Karla Linn Merrifield is a seven-time Pushcart-Prize nominee and National Park Artist-in-Residence. She has had some 400 poems appear in dozens of journals and anthologies. She has ten books to her credit, the newest of which are *Lithic Scatter and Other Poems* (Mercury Heartlink) and *Attaining Canopy: Amazon Poems* (FootHills Publishing). Forthcoming from Salmon Poetry is *Athabaskan Fractal and Other Poems of the Far North.* Her *Godwit: Poems of Canada* (FootHills) received the 2009 Eiseman Award for Poetry and she recently received the Dr. Sherwin Howard Award for the best poetry published in *Weber - The Contemporary West* in 2012. She is assistant editor and poetry book reviewer for *The Centrifugal Eye* (www.centrifugaleye.com), a member of the board of directors of TallGrass Writers Guild and Just Poets (Rochester, NY), and a member of the New Mexico State Poetry Society. Visit her blog, *Vagabond Poet,* at http://karlalinn.blogspot.com.

Claudia Messelodi works as a foreign language teacher at a high school. She has been writing poetry for many years. Some of her poems have been published both in national and international anthologies. She released her first poetry collection entitled "Sky-blue Wisteria. A poetic Journey" in March 2012 and her second collection "Variations of Sky and Soul" in March 2013.

Les Merton is Cornish and proud of it. He earned his living in a variety of ways: grocery shop manager, coalman, bus conductor, factory worker, canvasser, film extra, fortune teller, entertainment agent, and after failing as a comedian, the other jobs are best forgotten. He's dabbled at writing on and off from the age of 16, however it was in 1996 he decided to give it a go properly. In 2002, he founded Poetry Cornwall / Bardhonyeth Kernow and as been its editor ever since. In 2004, his endeavours were recognised when he was made a Bard of Gorsedh Kernow for services to Cornish Literature. His Bardic name is Map Hallow (Son of the Moors). He has also appear on: ITV's That Sunday

Night Show, BBC TV Spotlight News, and the following Radio Stations: BBC Radio Bristol, Duchy Hospital Radio, BBC Radio Cornwall, BBC Radio 4, Pirate FM, BBC Radio Five Live, ABC Radio Canberra Australia. He enjoys performing and has given readings all over the UK and in Ndola Zambia.

John Miatech has published three books of poetry, *Things to Hope For*, *Waiting for Thunder* and *What the Wind Says*. He currently is working on a new poetry collection, *Stretching into Evening*. Miatech's work has appeared in *Anesthesia Review*, *BlazeVox*, *RiverSedge*, *Cellar Roots*, *Big River Poetry Review*, *Savasvati*, *Blue Lake Review*, *Northwest Review*, and kindofahurricane. He received the poetry award at the San Francisco Literary Conference in 2012. John lives in Northern California, where he teaches high school. He grew up in Michigan.

George Moore has just had his fourth poetry collection, *The Hermits of Dingle* by FutureCycle Press; his fifth collection, *Children's Drawings of the Universe*, will be published by Salmon Poetry Press in 2014. Moore's poetry has appeared in The Atlantic, Poetry, North American Review, Colorado Review, and internationally. Nominated for Pushcart Prizes, Best of the Web and Net awards, he has been a recent finalist for The National Poetry Series, The Brittingham Award, and The Richard Snyder Poetry Prize. He lives with his wife, the Canadian poet, Tammy Armstrong, between Colorado and Nova Scotia.

Joseph Murphy has had poetry published in a number of journals, including *The Gray Sparrow*, *Third Wednesday* and *The Sugar House Review*. He is also a poetry editor for an online publication, *Halfway Down the Stairs*.

James B. Nicola, winner of three poetry awards and a Pushcart and Rhysling nominee, has published 350+ poems in *Atlanta Review*, *Tar River*, *Texas Review*, &c. A Yale grad and stage director by profession, his book *Playing the Audience* won a *Choice* Award. First full-length collection: "Manhattan Plaza" scheduled for 2014.

Christine Nichols is a new poet from Stillwater, Oklahoma.

George H. Northrup is President (2006-) of the Fresh Meadows Poets in Queens, NY, and a Board member of the Society that selects the Nassau County Poet Laureate. His poetry has been published in literary journals such as *Avocet, Buddhist Poetry Review, First Literary Review—East, Generations, Long Island Quarterly, Möbius, Oberon, Performance Poets Association Literary Review,* and *StepAway Magazine,* as well as in anthologies including *Bards Annual, Freshet, Long Island Sounds, Toward Forgiveness,* and *Writing Outside the Lines.* Five of his poems have been published in the *New York Times* Metropolitan Diary.

Bret Norwood is the author of a forthcoming collection of short stories called *Tales of the Credit Card Age.* His poetry has been published in *Open Window Review,* the *Owen Wister Review, Soundzine,* and other journals, and it has recently been recognized in the 2013 WyoPoets National and Members-Only contests.

Jennifer Ostromecki graduated from the University of Rochester with a bachelor's degree in British Literature and European History. Her poetry has appeared in Horrified Press' "Suffer Eternal: Volume One" and will be in the forthcoming "Suffer Eternal: Volume III." Her love of Victorian literature and Metaphysical poetry make her think she was born in the wrong century, but her fondness for social media begs to differ. Follow her: @jomecki.

Carl Palmer has been nominated twice for the Micro Award in flash fiction and thrice for the Pushcart Prize in poetry. He grew up on Old Mill Road in Ridgeway, VA. He now lives the good live in University Place, WA. His motto: Long Weekends Forever.

Stephen V. Ramey lives and writes in beautiful New Castle, Pennsylvania. His work has appeared in many places, most recently Gone Lawn, Crack the Spine, and Cactus Heart. His first collection of (very) short fiction, Glass Animals, is now available from Pure Slush Books. Find him at http://www.stephenvramey.com/

kerry rawlinson was born and raised in Africa, and spent almost four decades as a Canadian draftsman, designer, mother, wife. She's now redefining the latter half of her life as what she started out wanting to be as a young girl: poet, photographer and artist. Her first published works are in recent editions of Prospective: A Journal of Speculation, and upcoming in Ascent Aspirations' 2013 Anthology contest.

Nina Romano earned an M.A. from Adelphi University and an M.F.A. in Creative Writing from Florida International University. She is the author of three poetry collections: *Cooking Lessons* from Rock Press, submitted for the Pulitzer Prize, *Coffeehouse Meditations,* from Kitsune Books, and *She Wouldn't Sing at My Wedding*, from Bridle Path Press. Romano has been nominated twice for the Pushcart Prize. She co-authored *Writing in a Changing World.* Romano's chapbook, *Prayer in a Summer of Grace,* has just been published by Flutter Press. Her debut short story collection, *The Other Side of the Gates,* is forthcoming from Bridle Path Press. Her new poetry collection, *Faraway Confections,* is forthcoming from Kelsay Books. More about the author at: www.ninaromano.com

Eva Schlesinger is the author of the chapbooks, *Ode 2 Codes & Codfish* (slated for publication by dancing girl press in 2013), *View From My Banilla Vanilla Villa* (dancing girl press, 2010), and *Remembering the Walker and Wheelchair: poems of grief and healing* (Finishing Line Press, 2008). Her poetry also has received the *Literal Latte* Food Verse Award and aired on KPFA's (Pacifica Radio Network Affiliate) Cover To Cover Open Book. A native of Southeastern Connecticut beaches, she now lives in the Bay Area and visits the Pacific Ocean as often as she can. www.redroom.com/member/eva-schlesinger.

J.lynn Sheridan writes in the Chain O' Lakes of northern Illinois in a very ordinary house, but she'd rather live in an old hardware store for the aroma, ambiance, and possibilities. She has recently been published in *Beyond the Dark Room* and *Storm Cycle* 2012, Four and Twenty Literary Journal, The Plum Plum, Jellyfish Whispers,

MouseTales Press, and Enhance. She is currently working on her first novel. Find her at writingonthesun.wordpress.com and @J.lynnSheridan.

Tamara Simpson is a final-year music and science student at the University of Western Australia. She has had previous work published in the *Umbra Magazine*, the *Open Minds Magazine*, the *Everyday Poets Magazine*, the 2012 Best of Anthology *Storm Cycle* (by Kind of a Hurricane Press) and others. She hopes to pursue a career in writing.

Tom Sterner lives in Denver, Colorado with wife Kathy. He has been published in numerous magazines and on the internet, including *Howling Dog Press/Omega, Skyline Literary Review, The Storyteller, and Flashquake.* His internet pseudonym is WordWulf. A native of Colorado and proud father of five children and a stepdaughter, he writes lyrics, sings and composes music with his sons. He is winner of the Marija Cerjak Award for Avant-Garde/Experimental Writing and was nominated for the Pushcart Prize in 2006 and 2008. Published work includes two novels, *Madman Chronicles: The Warrior* and *Momma's Rain*.

Chris Stiebens is an English Professor and writer raised (all too humanly) in the rugged township of Manitou, Oklahoma. He now resides in Lawton, Oklahoma, where he noncommittally practices painting and birding. His true passions are his darling wife, Mary Elizabeth, their dogs, Squeaky and Maggie-Mae West, and the reading and crafting of well-rendered fiction. His most recent works have appeared in *The Subtopian* and *Corvus Magazine*. Any comments or questions about his story, 'Suddenly Sunday,' can be directed to his limited digital presence at stiebens@gmail.com.

Emily Strauss has an M.A. in English, but is self-taught in poetry. Over 100 of her poems appear in dozens of online venues and in anthologies. The natural world is generally her framework; she often focuses on the tension between nature and humanity, using concrete images to illuminate the loss of meaning between them.

She is a semi-retired teacher living near the Pacific Ocean in California.

Bonnie Quan Symons has had her poetry published in the Vancouver Courier, Four and Twenty, Resurrectionist Review, Translink Buzzer, and more recently, Skive Magazine. She has worked for the University of British Columbia and is currently working for the BC Teachers' Federation. She lives in Vancouver, British Columbia, Canada.

Marianne Szlyk is an associate professor of English at Montgomery College, Rockville, and an associate editor for Potomac Review. Several of her poems have appeared in Jellyfish Whispers. Others have appeared in Aberration Labyrinth, the Blue Hour Literary Magazine, and Ishaan Literary Review. She is inspired by urban and suburban nature and has fond memories of swimming in Maine, Lake Michigan, and the not-so new diving pool at Purdue.

Terence Thomas prefers to let his work speak for itself.

Tim Tobin holds a degree in mathematics from LaSalle University and is retired from L-3 Communications. His work appears in Static Movement, Cruentus Libri Press, The Speculative Edge, Rainstorm Press, Twisted Dreams, The Rusty Nail, In Parentheses, and the Whortleberry Press as well as various websites and ezines. He is a member of the South Jersey Writer's Group and of the Dead Poets Society of Camden County College.

Christine Tsen is a published cellist and poet. Her poems can be found in *THRUSH Poetry Journal, Montucky Review, Emerge,* and *The Bark.* So much of poetry feels like music, and music like poetry ~ and to her one lights up the other! Her philosophy is that every breath is a gift. More: www.ChristineThomasTsen.com.

Mercedes Webb-Pullman graduated from the International Institute of Modern Letters, Victoria University Wellington New Zealand with her MA in Creative Writing 2011. Her work as appeared in many online journals and collections, eBooks and in print. She lives on the Kapiti Coast, reads at open mic sessions there and in the city, and works for Lazarus Media LLC as Assistant Editor, Pacific, and Editor-in-Chief, DM du Jour.

Anne Whitehouse is a poet, fiction and non-fiction writer who lives in New York City. Her recollections of her childhood during the civil rights era in Birmingham, Alabama, may be read at Kids in Birmingham 1963. She was interviewed about her life and work in Harvard Stories. Her most recent poetry collection is The Refrain, published by Dos Madres Press in 2012. Other collections include The Refrain, Bear in Mind, One Sunday Morning, and The Surveyor's Hand. Her novel, Fall Love, is now available as an ebook from Feedbooks, Smashwords, Amazon Kindle, and iTunes. www.annewhitehouse.com

John Sibley Williams is the author of *Controlled Hallucinations* (FutureCycle Press, 2013) and six poetry chapbooks. He is the winner of the HEART Poetry Award, and finalist for the Pushcart, Rumi, and The Pinch Poetry Prizes. John serves as editor of *The Inflectionist Review*, co-director of the Walt Whitman 150 project, and Marketing Director of Inkwater Press. A few previous publishing credits include: *Third Coast, Nimrod International Journal, Inkwell, Cider Press Review, Bryant Literary Review, Cream City Review, The Chaffin Journal, The Evansville Review, RHINO,* and various anthologies. He lives in Portland, Oregon.

Martin Willitts, Jr. is a retired MLS Senior Librarian living in Syracuse, New York. He has an echapbook with Barometric Pressures: *"Late All Night Sessions with Charlie "the Bird" Parker and the Members of Birdland, in Take-Three"*(A Kind Of a Hurricane Press, ebook, 2013). His forthcoming poetry books include *"Waiting For The Day To Open Its Wings"* (UNBOUND Content, 2013), *"Art Is the Impression of an Artist"* (Edgar and Lenore's Publishing House, 2013), *"City Of Tents"* (Crisis Chronicles Press, 2013), "*A Is for Aorta*" (Seven Circles Press, e-book, 2013), "Swimming *In the Ladle of Stars*" (Kattywompus Press, 2013), and he is the winner of the inaugural Wild Earth Poetry Contest for his full length collection *"Searching For What Is Not There"* (Hiraeth Press, 2013).

Matthew Wylie currently lives in Canada and teaches European Literature at a small private school in North York, Ontario. Matthew's works have been published in various scholarly / poetry journals, such as *The Toronto Slavic Quarterly*, *Cinetext: Film and Philosophy*, *Temenos: Journal of Creative Writing*, *Ygdrasil: Journal of the Poetic Arts*, *International Zeitschrift*, *The Externalist: A Journal of Perspectives*, and others. He enjoys studying butterflies, entertaining the tigers that pace throughout the corridors of his home, photography, siestas, and sharks.

Robert Wynne earned his MFA in Creative Writing from Antioch University. A former co-editor of Cider Press Review, he has published 6 chapbooks, and 3 full-length books of poetry, the most recent being "Self-Portrait as Odysseus," published in 2011 by Tebot Bach Press. He's won numerous prizes, and his poetry has appeared in magazines and anthologies throughout North America. He lives in Burleson, TX with his wife, daughter and 3 rambunctious dogs. His online home is www.rwynne.com.

Ron Yazinski is a retired English teacher who, with his wife Jeanne, divides his time between Northeastern Pennsylvania and Winter Garden, Florida. His poems have appeared in Strong Verse, The Bijou Review, Amarillo Bay, The Edison Literary Review, The Cynic Review, The Wilderness House Review, Chantarelle's Notebook, The Electric Poet, Centrifugal Eye, amphibi.us, The Write Room, Pulsar and Crash. He is also the author of the chapbook *Houses: An American Zodiac*, which was published by The Poetry Library and a book of poems *South of Scranton*.

Mantz Yorke is a former teacher living in Manchester, England. His work has appeared in the series 'Best of Manchester Poets' and elsewhere.

About The Editors

A.J. Huffman has published five solo chapbooks and one joint chapbook through various small presses. Her sixth solo chapbook will be published in October by *Writing Knights Press*. She is a Pushcart Prize nominee, and the winner of the 2012 Promise of Light Haiku Contest. Her poetry, fiction, and haiku have appeared in hundreds of national and international journals, including *Labletter, The James Dickey Review, Bone Orchard, EgoPHobia, Kritya,* and *Offerta Speciale*, in which her work appeared in both English and Italian translation. She is also the founding editor of Kind of a Hurricane Press. www.kindofahurricanepress.com

April Salzano teaches college writing in Pennsylvania and is working on her first (several) poetry collections and an autobiographical work on raising a child with Autism. Her work has appeared in *Poetry Salzburg, Pyrokinection, Convergence, Ascent Aspirations, Deadsnakes, The Rainbow Rose, The Camel Saloon* and other online and print journals and is forthcoming in *Inclement, Poetry Quarterly, Bluestem* and *Rattle.*

Made in the USA
San Bernardino, CA
21 August 2013